The Ownership of All Life

Notes on Scandals, Conspiracies and Coverups

JON RAPPOPORT

TRUTH SEEKER
BOOKS SAN DIEGO, CALIFORNIA

**dedicated to Roy Tuckman
who rules the airwaves from midnight to 6am**

Introduction

In the buildup to World War 2, the Nazi cartel IG Farben engaged in a kind of mystical conjuring.

Farben had helped save Germany from final economic devastation after World War 1. It pioneered plastic fabrics and eliminated the need for Germany to go abroad for very expensive natural cloth. Farben's oil and rubber processing, in the 1930s, were years ahead of the rest of the world's technology.

The Farben executives began to believe they could synthesize anything. From anything.

They began to believe that they had the minds to see into the complete core of nature.

Just as Hitler and Himmler were devoted to the idea of synthesizing a new created race of superior people, Farben was beginning to believe its creative sway in the field of chemistry was without limit.

All this self-promoted arrogance was spun into the web of mystical Germanic philosophy. Somehow, these political and scientific fanatics thought, the German physical body with its "pure blood" was the best in the world, was what the world intended itself to be.

The attempt was to manage future bloodlines. Eugenics.

Many non-Germans were drawn into this bizarre invention of the super-race.

The current extreme fetishism about genes and genetic engineering plays right into this belief that blood is important. Never mind that current statements about genes drastically exaggerate the importance of those bits of coding. Genes in no way account for the overwhelming majority of important human traits or human actions or human choices. But once again we see people courting eugenics and bloodline-control.

Whether it is great sports figures, other celebrities, or the elites who run the world, millions of people want to know their secrets. And are falling into the trap of believing that, through genes, blood is central to the mystery of success, of talent, of intelligence.

People begin to think, subliminally, that success in life is arranged entirely as a gigantic crapshoot, and we can have no say in it. "It's all in the blood, in the genes."

"Maybe some day I can buy the genes I need, and then everything will change for me."

This is also the ultimate anti-history. Because the past and what happened in it are no longer considered of any use. What is useful is only physical manipulation of genetic structures. As that view spreads, the cruelty behind it will become more apparent.

After World War 2, the highest ranking scientist on the executive board of IG Farben, Dr. Fritz Ter Meer, was put on trial at Nuremburg. The charges? Mass slavery and murder.

Farben had built a rubber factory at Auschwitz. In fact, it built Auschwitz in order to ensure cheap labor in its adjoining rubber factory. Farben paid the SS to send over inmates every day to work in that factory. Those who were too weak to make it through the day were killed.

Well, for all this Fritz Ter Meer was given seven years in jail. A pathetic seven years.

... Sixteen years later, on August 1, 1963, the Bayer Corporation was celebrating its hundredth anniversary at Cologne. Big festivities.

The three largest original components of IG Farben— Bayer, Hoechst, and BASF—were back in business and roaring on profit highs. They were now sanitized separate corporations, no longer parts of an official Nazi-aiding IG Farben.

The keynote speaker at the Bayer celebration was the one and only Fritz Ter Meer.

Out of jail.

Murderer.

Mass murderer.

Now chairman of the supervisory board of Bayer.
Chairman. Of the Supervisory Board. Of Bayer.

1

Some of the most senior corporate and political leaders in America supported both sides in World War 2. This is not merely a fantasy. By reading, for example, as closely woven a book as Charles Higham's *Trading With the Enemy*, you would discover that ITT, through its shipments of vital parts to the Germans, made it possible for that war to exist at all.

At all.

But the denizens of the major media do not believe in conspiracy. They reserve that only for films and TV shows.

They do not bother to think that the transnational corporations which own staggering amounts of this world, and step on the faces of millions of foreign nationals, are a friend to every US president.

That is not important.

Because that is business as usual.

Because the salaries of media anchors and editors and news producers are paid by some of these transnationals, and therefore those who shape the news must become outraged and sanctimonious on other fronts.

2

Who were some of America's leading corporate lights who either supported Hitler, or supported both sides in the period leading up to and during World War 2?

The National City Bank, the Chase National Bank, Standard Oil of New Jersey, Ford Motor Co., ITT, General Motors, the Davis Oil Company. This is just the beginning.

Take Dean Acheson, who, during the Second World War, campaigned for the silent and, yes, conspiratorial continuation of the notorious Bank For International Settlements (BIS), a depository for Nazi millions. Acheson, later to become US Secretary of State, knew that laying open the truth about BIS would reveal that US banking leaders and British leaders were sitting on the board of that bank, part of whose assets came from melted down gold teeth and jewelry of concentration camp victims.

3

As persons on the political left and right become more exercised about each other—which is the root of the ongoing media circus—beyond that the biggest transnationals in the world continue to add to their assets. Their lands, their slave and cheap labor, their natural resources, their understandings with heads of state, their ties with intelligence agencies and military forces.

As of 1993, 300 transnationals controlled 25% of the world's productive capacity. (See *The Economist*, Mar. 27, 1993, "A Survey of Multinationals")

This is reality.

Monsanto, Dow, Du Pont, Bayer, Hoechst, Rhone Poulenc, Imperial Chemical Industries, and Novartis are all researching and growing genetically engineered crops which have the supreme quality of being able to absorb and tolerate more of the parent company's (specific) pesticides without curling up and dying in the fields.

Pesticide drenched fields.

And drenched bodies of those who eat the foods.

No word from this administration about this. The Clinton White House is, in fact, enthusiastic about genetically engineered (GE) food. Or, as the government calls it, GMOs, genetically modified organisms.

There is no official US insistence that such foods be labeled or identified in any way. Because these GEs are said to be identical or equivalent to natural food. That is the fiat.

You're already eating genetically engineered soy beans from Monsanto.

You're soaking in it.

You're soaking in the power of transnationals to shape the world, to select its genes.

But it's not a significant story on the evening news.

4

Monsanto manufactures and sells Bovine Growth Hormone (BGH), the genetically engineered biological that makes cows produce more milk.

For health reasons (their cows get sick with mastitis infections, need more antibiotics, and then the medicine and pus can seep into the milk supply), farmers all over the world have been up in arms about BGH, and yet the US government has steadfastly refused to support labeling milk BGH-free when it is. (Canada has just banned the use of BGH.)

The mastitis and its consequences for the milk supply, as indicated above, were obvious to Monsanto from its own studies on BGH.

An employee of the FDA (1985-88), Dr. Richard Burroughs had the job of checking data supplied by Monsanto and other companies who were testing BGH with hopes of marketing it. He decided that the books were being cooked, that data were being falsified. He went to Congress and told them this, and he also said that his bosses at the FDA were covering up these lies. In 1989 he was fired.

In the revealing book, *Toxic Sludge Is Good For You*, John Stauber writes, "Monsanto was the manufacturer of most of the world's PCBs—persistent chemicals used in electrical equipment which have been shown to cause cancer and birth defects. It is also the world's largest producer of herbicides, including products contaminated with dioxin [thought to be the world's most toxic small molecule]."

5

The fact that a politician supports to one degree or another the agendas of transnationals is not even on the charts. It is not even a talking point. It is not an issue. It is not a blip on the screen of the western world.

Being that these transnationals are the most powerful aggregate on the planet, one would think that a politician's attitude toward them would be noticed, important.

Why isn't it?

Because.

Because some things are successfully hidden.

In 1989, Du Pont puts 250 million pounds of industrial wastes into the earth by the deep injection method. Like drilling for oil, except you PUT extremely toxic substances there, to drift horizontally, to come up into the water table.

This fact about Du Pont is at least as important as bombing strikes on Iraq.

But no one is told that.

No one makes that kind of dumping weird and foul and crazy enough to be on the news every night.

6

How do GE food and BGH and massive dumping of industrial pollutants assume a benign character? Through false science, through "studies" which assert that everything is all right.

This science is beneficial to corporations who have a huge profit-stake in how their products are viewed vis-a-vis safety and efficacy.

How far could fraud go in this? How bizarre and destructive could false science be? How widely accepted could groundless research become?

In 1991, the Group for the Scientific Reappraisal of HIV, based in San Diego, collected over 300 signatures, the majority of them from scientists, at the bottom of a very spare letter, which simply said:

"It is widely believed by the general public that a retrovirus called HIV causes the group of diseases called AIDS. Many biochemical scientists now question the hypothesis. We propose that a thorough reappraisal of the existing evidence for and against this hypothesis be conducted by a suitable independent group. We further propose that critical epidemiological studies be devised and undertaken."

They had some very prominent scientists as signers. Two Nobel laureates.

But forget stimulating the funding of new research. They couldn't even get the letter PUBLISHED in a reputable medical journal. Not *Nature*. Not *Science*. Not the *New England Journal*. Not *The Lancet*.

That's how tight the wagons of consensus were circled against them.

Kary Mullis, Nobel laureate in chemistry, has pointed out, many times, an incredibly corrosive fact: "There is no single published journal paper which proves that HIV causes AIDS. It does not exist. It never did."

The day after Robert Gallo announced on national television that he had found the cause of AIDS (spring, 1984), all government monies which had been granted to support research into the cause of AIDS evaporated. Now the grants had to be about finding out the mechanism by which HIV caused AIDS.

That's how research and publication of alternative views on AIDS causation were chilled.

That's how the fear among researchers was instilled.

No honorable researcher in his right mind would accept: science by press conference/and a lack of a journal paper which proves HIV causes AIDS. That is unthinkable, particularly when people are dying all over the world.

But it happened.

Came the march of the cowards.

ABC did several shows on this issue of HIV. I was interviewed for one of them, a *Nightline* piece in 1994. It was clear that Koppel was angered by the apparent lying that had gone on in the name of science at the highest levels.

But then ABC dropped the whole thing, as if it had never existed. A story far more potent in its implications, and more scandalous, than Watergate.

ABC eventually realized that three quiet separate federal investigations of Robert Gallo had been undertaken. Into possible criminality vis-a-vis his research on HIV. But even that didn't budge them into pushing this story into orbit.

The thousands of federal pages that were compiled on Gallo's strange activities were eventually shelved by the Clinton administration. Pages, for example, on Gallo's outright theft of French viral research.

7

I had written a book, *AIDS INC.*, in 1988, in which I said that HIV had never been proved to cause AIDS. I found so many contradictions in the research picture of HIV, it was like probing the mind of a rampant dyslexic—albeit one acting with arrogance and surety.

One of the key conversations I had in writing *AIDS INC.* was with Jay Levy, widely accepted as a world-class AIDS researcher.

I said, "How do we know that HIV causes AIDS? Where is the proof?"

He said without pause, "We know it because if you transfuse a healthy person with blood that contains HIV he gets AIDS and dies."

I found that remark astonishing. I did a little checking around.

Here is what I wrote in *AIDS INC.*, in 1988: "Calculating from figures supplied by the American Association of Blood Banks, since 1978 about 29 million Americans have received blood transfusions. In most of these transfusions, more than one donor supplied the various pints injected, so there was ample opportunity to receive HIV in the bloodstream. The average size of a transfusion is 3.5 pints.

"As of February 1988, the CDC reports a total of 1466 transfusion-AIDS cases in the US (since AIDS was first reported). This means that about .00005 of those who have received transfusions in the last ten years have been diagnosed with AIDS. That's 5 thousandths of one percent.

"On that basis, could you possibly infer that HIV is the cause of something called AIDS? Obviously not. One could argue that these statistics don't absolutely rule out HIV ...

but this is not the question."

So a top AIDS researcher told me how everybody knows that HIV causes AIDS. What he told me made about as much sense as Jerry Springer on acid.

8

But the American public has bought that explanation.

This reminds me of DeNiro's remark to Dustin Hoffman in *Wag the Dog*: "They showed one smart bomb going down inside a building. That one thing, and the public bought the whole [Iraq] war."

How does a medical researcher prove that a germ causes a disease?

That's a damn good question.

The closer you look, the weirder it gets.

The researcher has something called Koch's postulates. As full of holes as this method is, it has often been cited as the way medical researchers find out what is behind a new disease.

In the case of AIDS, you would remove and isolate HIV from several humans who have been diagnosed with the syndrome, and you would inject that into animals. If you saw the illness symptoms develop in EVERY ONE of those animals, you would know you were on the right track.

With AIDS, monkeys in a number of facilities have been used. The results have been zero. Over the last decade and more, the 150 or so primates have failed to show full-blown symptoms.

Of course, there are comebacks for this, and they have all been used.

"Let's wait another twenty years."

"We'll keep these damn monkeys out of their natural habitat long enough and their immune systems will finally collapse and they'll show AIDS-like symptoms."

"Monkeys just don't get AIDS."

"Let's wait thirty years."

"Two monkeys got the flu. That's good enough."

Point is, the traditional method failed.

So then the most oft used backup method is correlation. Take a group of people who have been diagnosed as HIV positive, and who do not have serious illnesses, and follow them over a period of time. Do they come down with the symptoms of what is being called AIDS?

The biggest group used in this respect is the San Francisco Men's study, which began as a hepatitis B study in 1978. Several thousand men have been part of this cohort, as it's called.

Researchers, when pressed, point to this as the best evidence that HIV causes AIDS. But there is a serious flaw or two. Although a large number of men who were HIV positive went on to develop illnesses called AIDS, the study did only spotty tracking on men who never tested positive for HIV.

One of the researchers on the San Francisco study told me frankly that HIV negative men could have developed AIDS-defining diseases when they were not being tracked. In which case, positive or negative would not be the defining indication of AIDS.

What this researcher didn't say was this:

The San Francisco Men's Study showed that an extraordinary number of men, diagnosed as HIV positive, simply by not taking the drug AZT had remained healthy for ten years.

AZT happens to attack the bone marrow, where certain cells of the immune-system are manufactured.

A surprise group of HIV-positive men who stayed healthy for ten years or more had not taken AZT or had stopped taking it.

This fact was not trumpeted by the San Francisco Study.

9

Immune-system breakdown, after a certain point, has the same general appearance in people, regardless of the cause: whether we are talking about starvation and dirty water in

Africa and Vietnam, immune-suppressing vaccines all over the Third World, pesticides in the American south, multiple-drug use in the bath houses of San Francisco, a possibly immune-system-destroying hepatitis B vaccine delivered experimentally to gay men in several cities of America, the immense overuse of antibiotics for years among a group of gay men in San Francisco and New York (brought about by unscrupulous physicians), or the incredibly toxic drug AZT.

Immune-system breakdown allows bizarre and rare infections to occur, from germs that ordinarily would cause no harm. That is how people get pneumocystis pneumonia, for example, called the primary symptom of AIDS. This micro-organism is naturally present in perhaps 75% of people all over the world. It does nothing. But like other germs, if the immune system collapses entirely, FROM VARIOUS CAUSES, it comes to the fore and begins to overmultiply. Therefore pneumocystis pneumonia was found among ill-fed and orphaned children in eastern Europe or among starving children at makeshift orphanages in Vietnam during the war.

10

Dream monologue.

"As CEO of one of the largest drug corporations in the world, one of the largest organizations of any kind in the history of the world, I can say that I buy time on Dan Rather for more than profit. More than promotion. I buy it to support what this country really stands for: a central source of information that has the capacity to convince the American people that what is going on is THIS NOT THAT. Every night it is this. Not that. This. When you stop and think about it, it's a wondrous thing. Without bludgeons, without narcotics, without duress, without torture, we have found a way to keep the perception of the average person on various rails. Within certain limits. In certain boxes. I support that whole-heartedly because I know that it strengthens my world and my goddamn grip on people. For example, I realize perfectly

well—because I've made it my business to learn the truth—
that AIDS is really a collection of different forms of immune-
suppression from different causes around the world. I know
that the causes in many cases are chemical, or relate to horrible
starvation in the Third World. But my company makes no
money from that. There is no medical drug we can develop
to treat that. We have to have the mirage of a single medical
condition caused by a single germ. THEN we can find a drug
and a vaccine and sell them. In the case of AIDS, we saw
AZT come to the fore as the drug of choice, and billions of
dollars of profit were made. The AIDS vaccine, if it ever comes
to market, could mean profits of two or three hundred billion
dollars. For that kind of money, we need to maintain our
position in people's minds as the authorities in the field of
disease. We have to present ourselves and advertise and use
the best channels of information to dominate minds. Let me
make this clear. I know that in the process of manipulating
the truth people will suffer. People will die. People that could
be cured of disease will be treated with the wrong thing and
they will die. The real causes of their immune-suppression
will be overlooked, will not be removed. But since we're being
candid, let me tell you that the fate of people at large is not
my concern, no matter what public pronouncements I make.
Whether numbers of people die is immaterial, because the
species still survives. That's how I look at it. Not everyone
can be saved. I believe that the people who will survive deep
into the next century will deserve to live. Their bloodlines
will go on because they fought the hardest, they learned how
to compete, they gave up unworkable ideas. Elimination of
groups of people is one of the events of history and who
wants to fight history?"

1 1

As William Burroughs used to say, "This is reality. You
and a few friends get some uniforms and guns and set up a
glass booth on a lonely road in Mexico. You call it an official
government checkpoint and every car that comes by you step

out and stop it and collect the tax."

In 1798, Thomas Malthus, the famous British economist, wrote his *Essay on the Principle of Population.* As a forerunner of those elitists who would take up the banner of good and bad genes and selective breeding and depopulation of nations, Malthus wrote these astonishing words, at the dawn of the industrial revolution:

"... if we dread the too frequent visitation of the horrid form of famine, we should sedulously encourage the other forms of destruction, which we compel nature to use. Instead of recommending cleanliness to the poor, we should encourage contrary habits. In our towns we should make the streets narrower, crowd more people into the houses, and court the return of the plague. In the country, we should build our villages near stagnant pools, and particularly encourage settlements in all marshy and unwholesome situations. But above all, we should reprobate [disapprove of as immoral] specific remedies for ravaging diseases; and [also disapprove of] those benevolent, but much mistaken men, who have thought they were doing a service to mankind by projecting schemes for the total extirpation of particular disorders."

Although we tend to think that all the disgusting interpretations of Charles Darwin's work which led to more ideas about eugenics and "pruning down" the human race came from interpreters of Darwin's research, this is a distortion. Darwin himself was an admirer of Malthus, whom he took as a major stated influence.

Darwin wrote: "With the savages, the weak in body or mind are soon eliminated; and those that survive commonly exhibit a vigorous state of health. We civilised men, on the other hand, do our utmost to check the process of elimination; we build asylums for the imbecile, the maimed and the sick; we institute poor-laws; and our medical men exert their utmost skill to save the life of every one to the last moment. There is reason to believe that vaccination has preserved thousands, who from a weak constitution would formerly have succumbed to smallpox. Thus the weak members of civilised societies propagate their kind. No one who has attended to the breeding of domestic animals will doubt that this must be highly injurious to the race of man. It is surprising how soon ... care wrongly directed, leads to the degeneration of a domestic race; but excepting in the case of man himself, hardly any one is so ignorant as to allow his worst animals to breed."

In a letter to William Graham, Darwin followed this line of thinking: "Looking at the world at no very distant date, what an endless number of the lower races will have been eliminated by the higher civilised races throughout the world."

12

Alongside genocide and depopulation, you can place the program of turning the world of human beings into a kind of machine, a kind of ant colony, a collection of ant colonies.

That is the world we are drifting into, which will be run (to a greater extent than now) by the transnationals.

The individual human being is considered expendable by the overwhelming majority of elitists who run the global economy.

We should understand that the eugenics program forwarded by the Nazis was a public outbreak of a philosophy which has been held close to the vest by the "big boys" for many decades.

To insert the right amount of chill in the air at this point, read the words of Richard Barnet and John Cavanaugh, authors of the disturbing expose, *Global Dreams: Imperial Corporations and the New World Order,* as they uncover the crowning statement from the paradigm that says the world is a only a marketplace and the corporations own it:

"There is much data that points to a stark reality: A huge and increasing proportion of human beings are not needed and will never be needed to make goods or to provide services because too many people in the world are too poor to buy them."

As long as we persist in thinking of the world as a gigantic mall, we are courting genocide on a scale that has never been visited on the human race.

13

The best analyses of the history of disease on this planet have come to the conclusion that clean water, improved sanitation, better food, higher standard of living, the growth of a middle class have been the overriding factors in the decline of the bulk of human disease over time. Not antibiotics, not vaccines, not other drugs, not surgery, not hospitals.

It is the job of the American Medical Association to focus attention toward the drugs and surgery and vaccines, even though the basic core of the doctor's oath is to heal by using whatever will heal.

Medical societies are in the business of asserting that germs are our real problem, not starvation, not contaminated drinking water in the Third World, not toxic industrial and agri chemicals, not any of the obvious causes of illness and death.

The American Medical Association, since 1975, has channeled somewhere in the vicinity of $75 million into its own political action committee, the American Medical Political Action Committee (AMPAC).

This money is funneled through to favored candidates who run for office all over the US.

The federal watchdog agency whose job it is to keep PACs like AMPAC honest is the Federal Election Commission (FEC).

The FEC has its Washington offices in a building at 999 E Street, NW.

The building is owned by the American Medical Association.

In 1986, the AMA rolled its AMPAC money machine up to the door of a man named David Williams, who was running for a seat in the US Congress then occupied by Pete Stark, a Demo from California. The AMA wanted to get rid of Stark because he was not supporting AMA interests to the greatest degree possible in his position as the chair of a health committee.

AMPAC spent more than $250,000 on behalf of David Williams.

Out of nowhere.

Stark went to the FEC and complained.

The FEC declined to investigate the massive intervention by the AMA's PAC.

At that time, the head of the FEC was Lee Ann Elliot, who had once worked in a high position for the AMA. In fact, she was still getting a pension from the AMA.

In the FEC's internal vote to decide whether to investigate Congressman Stark's complaint, Lee Ann Elliot's NO ballot was the determining one.

14

Since 1954 in the United States, the administration of one class of twenty psychiatric drugs called neuroleptics— Thorazine, Haldol, Mellaril, Stelazine, Prolixin, and others— has caused between 300,000 and one million cases of motor brain damage.

There is no medical drug that can treat THAT.

15

Every year in the United States, physicians perform 15 million unnecessary surgeries. Every year, 60,000 people die from those unnecessary surgeries.

No germ causes THAT.

16

In 1991, three British scientists wrote a paper.

The paper was about the effects of BGH (aka rBGH, BST,

Bovine Growth Hormone), a genetically engineered hormone, on the cows it was being given to by Monsanto Corporation. Monsanto was testing the hormone, prior to trying to gain governments' approval for marketing it around the world.

BGH makes cows produce more milk.

"Good for business."

"Yep."

The three scientists, Erik Millstone, Eric Brunner, and Ian White had been analyzing data on BGH for Monsanto.

These researchers were not happy.

They said Monsanto had blocked publication of their paper.

Well, their paper stated that cows injected with BGH were experiencing an infection called mastitis, and this was elevating pus and bacteria counts in the cows.

The implication was clear.

The pus would find its way into the milk that consumers drank. And the increased amounts of antibiotics which would be used to treat the mastitis would seep into the milk, and consumers would drink that too.

Bad.

Monsanto forbade these three men from publishing their paper.

17

A Washington-based public interest group, the Foundation on Economic Trends, obtained secret documents, which it gave to the *New York Times.*

These documents show one of the roads Monsanto walked to try to get US government approval to market BGH to dairy farmers.

The President of Monsanto, Robert B. Shapiro, asked a man named Tony Coehlo for help.

Coehlo is a former congressman from California "and house majority whip who left that post in 1989 amid accusations that he had improperly used his political contacts to arrange and finance a $100,000 junk-bond investment for himself. Coehlo became a New York investment banker and, because he remained very-well connected, President Clinton selected him as chief strategist for the Democratic National Committee in 1994."

Coehlo had major connections at the US Department of Agriculture. The Agriculture Secretary, Mike Espy, had run for Congress in 1986, and had received $ for his race from the Democratic Congressional Campaign Committee— whose chief was Tony Coehlo. In fact later on, Clinton had chosen Espy as Secretary of Agriculture after a recommendation from Coehlo.

The stage was set for a dinner chat between Espy and Coehlo.

In fact, an employee at Monsanto, Dr. Virginia Weldon, on Sept. 23, 1993, wrote a memo entitled, "Coehlo Talking Points for Espy Dinner." Among the talking points was the following: "Let Secretary Espy know that companies like Monsanto will likely pull out of the agriculture biotech area [e.g. BGH] if the Administration will not stand up to persons like Senator Feingold."

Russ Feingold had put together opposition in Congress to BGH. Feingold wanted a study to be done which would analyze what increased milk production for the big dairy farmers would do to the small farmers and to the milk market in general—as in glut.

BGH increases milk production in cows.

The Weldon memo called for an attempt to get around any desire in Congress to do a "social impact" study of BGH. Leon Panetta was mentioned as the man to contact.

The Foundation on Economic Trends, which had uncovered this memo, released its contents, and the dinner chat between Coehlo and Espy never came off.

But BGH was approved by the FDA for use and it went to market in late 1993.

Three members of Congress then accused Monsanto of a fix. The Government Accounting Office did a study, which cleared Monsanto of any wrongdoing.

—This, despite the fact that the report said three FDA officials involved in approving BGH were former Monsanto players.

Ex-Monsanto lawyer Michael Taylor, ex-Monsanto scientist Margaret Miller, and a student of Monsanto researcher Suzanne Sechen.

In November 1994, the Canadian Broadcasting Company aired an episode of its show, *Fifth Estate,* which stated that Monsanto had attempted to bribe the Canadian FDA for up to $2 million—if Monsanto got a green light to market BGH in Canada.

Reporters for Fifth Estate claim that Monsanto tried to get the show stopped.

Later, Canadian government scientists stated that the US FDA had made an invalid decision to release BGH in the US. Essentially, the Canadian scientists claimed that the FDA had misreported vital data on studies and thereby led the public to a false rosy picture of the hormone.

The reply by the US FDA spokesman, John Scheid, was astonishing. As far as the data in question were concerned, he said, the FDA had never seen them. They had only seen a summary of the key study provided by Monsanto.

In other words, Monsanto had run a study which asserted that BGH was safe, and it provided a summary of that study (no raw data, no methods and procedures) to the FDA and the FDA had swallowed it whole with no questions.

The Canadian scientists who blew the whistle on the US FDA had even more to say. They pointed out that in the case of BGH, "The usually required long-term toxicology studies to ascertain human safety were not conducted. Hence, such possibilities and potential as sterility, infertility, birth defects, cancer, and immunological derangements were not addressed."

Welcome to the other side of the looking glass.

Two authors of this Canadian report, plus four other Canadian scientists, have said they were threatened with job-transfers, "where they would never be heard from again," unless they got down to serious work bringing approval for BGH in Canada. These scientists were ordered not to talk to reporters, but in government testimony sessions they made it clear that the Canadian FDA was groveling for Monsanto and saying the hell with good science and good health.

18

Monsanto and other giant corporations have grabbed on to a legal strategy which allows them to minimize losses from suits filed by consumers of their products.

Monsanto, for example, can bring a drug/hormone like BGH to market with less worries because a judge named Jack Weinstock made a crucial and strange ruling in the case of Vietnam vets asking damages from Dow, Monsanto, and Diamond Shamrock in the famous Agent Orange case.

The ruling is this: once a damage case is settled for a sum with all the plaintiffs, there can be no more suits filed on that issue, that product, even if new consumers surface who have never heard of the original settlement.

Completely contrary to due process, this judgement means that the usual progress of suits on top of suits is curtailed, and the offending company will not be subjected to higher and higher damages as new successive evidence is uncovered of their crimes and their knowledge of those crimes and their coverups.

19

A story was scheduled to be aired on Tampa Bay TV station WTVT, a Fox affiliate. The date was February 24, 1997.

Two seasoned reporters, Steve Wilson and Jane Akre, had finished a four-part look at Monsanto and its BGH product.

The series was going to be critical of Monsanto.

On Feb. 21, the head of Fox news, Roger Ailes, found a letter in his tray from a lawyer named John Walsh of the firm Cadwalader, Wickersham, and Taft. The firm had been hired by Monsanto.

The letter stated that Monsanto felt the series was going to be unfairly slanted against the company. "There is a lot at stake," Walsh wrote, "not only for Monsanto, but also for Fox News and its owner."

Executives at WTVT checked over the series and found no errors. They offered to re-interview Monsanto people for the series. After dialogue about this possibility, Monsanto objected to the accusatory sense of some of the topics and questions that would be re-covered. Lawyer Walsh fired off a threat— "... some of the points clearly contain the elements of defamatory statements which, if repeated in a broadcast, could lead to serious damage to Monsanto and dire consequences to Fox News."

Now came a flood of Fox-ordered rewrites. Reporters Wilson and Akre became very uncomfortable with changes in their series. Suddenly the credentials of scientists who had come out against Monsanto were left out of the piece. A quote from one of these researchers, "We're going to save lives if we review this [BGH] now," was deleted. IGF-1, a growth factor (and promoter of cancer) that is found at higher levels in BGH-treated milk, was no longer mentioned by name. The word "cancer" was changed to "human health implications." Florida grocers, in the original script, had been exposed for going back on their promise not to sell BGH-milk until it had gained wide approval. In the new script, these grocers were no longer criticized, they were complimented, as if they had decided to sell BGH-milk because consumers wanted them to.

Akre and Wilson state that they were ordered to delete information about Monsanto's past bad actions.

Akre and Wilson say that a new statement was added to their script: "This [BGH] is the most studied molecule certainly in the history of domestic animal science." The reporters felt this was a false depiction—and of course it implied that BGH was safe.

In fact, there were no long-term human studies of "the most studied molecule" before FDA approval to sell it in milk—and there was no order to label commercial milk as containing BGH.

"The consumer doesn't need to have a choice."

"The consumer is too stupid to know how to judge these things."

"What's important is the corporation, not the consumer."

Tremendous pressure from Fox came down, Akre and Wilson state.

Wilson says that when he and Akre responded to a threat of firing by mentioning that they would then file a formal complaint with the FCC, "We were not fired but were each offered very large cash settlements to go away and keep quiet about the story and how it was handled."

After much continued pressure, Akre and Wilson report that they were suspended without pay and locked out of their offices, where all their information on the BGH story was kept. This was October of 1997, eight months after the series was to have been aired.

On December 2, the reporters were fired by Fox.

20

Think. For every toxic substance—whether food ingredient or medical drug or pesticide or industrial chemical—released on the public, there must be a supporting background of false research accepted through criminal negligence, at the least, by official government agencies.

Here is a quote from Ross Brockley, writing in that national treasure of a magazine, the *Multinational Monitor*, July/August 1991. In this case, even government action against a massively toxic chemical is not enough to stop a corporation dedicated to depraved indifference to human life:

"The EPA ordered a freeze-out of [Dow Corporation's pesticide ingredient] DBCP on food and later banned all pesticides containing the substance. The action came after DBCP contaminated ground water in an area of thousands of square miles in the central valley of California and made agricultural workers who were exposed to it sterile. Aware of the pesticide's devastating effects, Dow sold much of its stockpile of DBCP to the Dole Corporation which used it on banana plantations in Costa Rica."

21

Under the aegis of the Dow Corporation, the pharmaceutical house Marion Merrell Dow brought to market Clomid, a drug that attempts to produce ovulatory stimulation so that pregnancy can occur in women for whom that would otherwise be unlikely.

In clinical trials, 7578 patients took Clomid. 2835 pregnancies were reported. 2369 of these pregnancies were then tracked. An astounding 483 spontaneous abortions occurred. There were also 24 stillbirths.

From the *Physician's Desk Reference*, here is a partial list of Clomid's post-marketing effects: seizure, stroke, psychosis, cataracts, posterior vitreous detachment, arrhthymia, tachycardia, hepatitis, liver and breast and pituitary and ovarian and kidney and tongue and bladder cancer, brain abscess, tubal pregnancy, uterine hemorrhage, ovarian hemorrhage. In the babies born to the mothers taking Clomid, there have occurred neuroectodermal tumor, thyroid tumor, leukemia, abnormal bone development including skeletal malformations of the skull and face and nasal passages and jaw and hand and limb and foot and joints, malformations of the anus and eye and lens and ear and lung and heart and genitalia, dwarfism, deafness, mental retardation, chromosomal disorders, neural tube defects.

22

70,000 people are hospitalized, and 7000 die in a year, from the effects of NSAIDS (Non-Steroidal Anti-Inflammatory Drugs). Some of these drugs are available over the counter for arthritis. (*Journal of Rheumatology*, 1991, Supplement 28, Volume 18, "NSAID Gastropathy," James Fries)

23

A parallel statistic: (published in *Rx For Better Health*, EJ Phelps and Company, San Diego, summer 1997, citing a US Drug Enforcement Agency statistic) In 1995, heroin caused 74,000 emergency room visits and 4000 deaths.

Not quite as lethal as NSAIDS.

24

The last overall report done on the field of medical practice in the United States was published in 1978. It was "Assessing the Efficacy and Safety of Medical Technologies," put together and researched by Congress' own Office of Technology Assessment (OTA). This United States Department of Commerce Document, PB-286929, dated September 1978, states in summary, "It has been estimated that only 10-20% of all procedures currently used in medical practice have been shown to be efficacious by controlled trial."

25

"Today the Swiss company Hoffman-LaRoche is the world's leading seller of legal psychotrtopic drugs ... [its former president] Elmer Bobst revealed that La Roche was heavily involved in the supply of morphine to the underworld between the two wars ... The Canton Road smuggling case heard by the mixed court of Shanghai in 1925 revealed the extensive involvement of Hoffman-LaRoche in the illegal drug trade. The case involved 180 chests of opium ... and 26 boxes containing mostly heroin imported from Basle, Switzerland, by a Chinese dealer, Gwando...

"... At the 1923 meeting of the Opium Advisory Committee, the Chinese representative pointed out that [pharmaceutical companies in] Germany, Great Britain, Switzerland, and the United States were all turning out 'morphine by the ton, which was purchased by smugglers by the ton.'"

26

Here are two anecdotes from the landmark 1990 report "Biotechnology's Bitter Harvest," published by researchers of the Bio-Technology Working Group, under a grant from the CS Fund and several other funds and foundations:

"When American Cyanamid developed a new family of imidazolinone herbicides, it contracted with Molecular Genetics to find a gene that would give crops tolerance to these chemicals [tolerance equals the ability of crops to absorb, without dying, increased amounts of these toxic chemicals]. Once the gene had been identified, Cyanamid gave it [the gene], gratis, to Pioneer Hi-Bred—the world's largest corn breeding company. Pioneer has agreed to insert the gene into its hybrids—much to the benefit of Cyanamid (*AgBiotechnology News*, 1985)."

"According to Plant Genetic Systems (a Belgian biotechnology company), development of crops tolerant to Hoechst's Basta [an herbicide] would increase the herbicide's global sales by $200 million a year..."

27

For many years, patients and researchers have asserted that medical treatments for diseases can begin a dangerous cycle of more toxic drugs given for the "side-effects" of the original treatment.

Here is a study which reveals how that can happen in a specific area.

The New England Journal of Medicine, on January 4, 1990 published a paper by John Kaldor, PhD, et al, titled "Leukemia Following Hodgkins Disease." The abstract states, "We conclude that chemotherapy for Hodgkins disease greatly increases the risk of leukemia and that this increased risk appears to be dose-related..."

28

In the autumn of 1970, the Japanese government banned the use of all medical drugs in Japan which contained the compound called clioquinol. These antidiarrheal drugs were manufactured by the Swiss chemical giant, Ciba-Geigy, under a variety of names.

More than 11,000 people in Japan had suffered from the effects of clioquinol between 1955 and 1970. Some of the symptoms: numbness, blindness, paralysis, death.

There was a smokescreen between clioquinol and the Japanese discovering that the drug was the cause of what was being called subacute myelo-optic neuropathy (SMON). The medical establishment was bent in the direction of looking for germs.

Eventually, through the courageous work of several researchers and a lawyer, the truth was exposed.

Ciba knew as early as 1935 that there were serious problems with clioquinol. Reports had come in from Argentina, where the compound had been introduced as an oral preparation for the first time. The same symptoms as later surfaced in Japan were being cited in Argentina.

Poisoning.

That's what was taking place.

Animal tests—as misleading as they are—are relied on by pharmaceutical companies. In the case of clioquinol, Ciba found in the late 1930s that cats were convulsing and sometimes dying from the drug. Dogs were dying from seizures.

Dr. Olle Hansson, a Swedish researcher, published a paper in *The Lancet* in 1966, linking optic atrophy and blindness to clioquinol.

Ciba did nothing.

Victims of the drug in Japan began to sue Ciba in 1972. It took 6 years to wring an apology and $ damages out of the company.

Ciba issued a press release in 1980 on SMON, saying "there

is no conclusive evidence that clioquinol causes SMON." In fact, the company continued to manufacture and sell drugs containing clioquinol in other countries.

Ciba dragged its feet until 1985, at which time it stopped manufacturing clioquinol for oral use.

But there are, as of 1993, still a large number of drugs sold around the world which contain clioquinol or related toxic compounds, and a number of companies are making profits and poisoning people with both oral preparations and creams.

In writing the book *AIDS INC.* in 1987, I found a number of cases in which AIDS was being used as a label to cover groups of people who were suffering with "AIDS-like illness" as a result of their ingesting toxic pharmaceuticals.

I have no doubt that this has happened in the Third World with clioquinol and related drugs.

In Haiti, for example, a clioquinol spin-off has been sold for gastrointestinal problems.

It's important to understand that many major chemical corporations, the giants, have separate divisions that produce pharmaceuticals, pesticides, genetically engineered food seeds, and industrial products (e.g., toxic PVC plastics, used universally for pipes—Dow is perhaps the largest producer of PVC in the world).

The eight largest pesticide companies in the world are, or are owned by, Monsanto, Dow, Du Pont, Imperial Chemical Industrial Industries (England), Rhone Poulenc (France), Ciba-Geigy (Switzerland—now Novartis), Bayer and Hoescht (Germany). Bayer is often ranked, from year to year, as the biggest chemical company in the world.

Each of these corporations has pharmaceutical divisions, industrial chemical divisions, genetically engineered food divisions.

29

As I began this book by saying, certain corporations do more than produce toxic products. They promote wars which are good for business, or which will establish their grip on foreign countries.

Smedley Butler enlisted in the US Marines in 1898. After moving all the way up to Major General, he was almost court-martialed in 1931. He retired. He joined The League Against War and Fascism. He wrote a book, *War is a Racket.*

Here is a fragment from a speech he gave in 1933. It offers the unique perspective of a loyal soldier who sees more than just a nationalistic or jingoistic slant on war.

"I wouldn't go to war again as I have done to protect some lousy investment of the bankers.

"... I helped make Mexico, especially Tampico, safe for American oil interests in 1914. I helped make Hawaii and Cuba a decent place for the National City Bank boys to collect revenues in. I helped in the raping of half a dozen Central American republics for the benefits of Wall Street. The record of racketeering is long. I helped purify Nicaragua for the international banking house of Brown Brothers in 1909-1912. I brought light to the Dominican Republic for American sugar interests in 1916. In China I helped see to it that Standard Oil went its way unmolested.

"During those years, I had, as the boys in the back room would say, a swell racket. I was rewarded with honors, medals and promotions. Looking back on it, I feel that I could have given Al Capone a few hints. The best he could do was to operate his racket in three districts. I operated on three continents."

30

These days we have ignorant and sold-out people arguing on both sides of the military-spending issue.

If the US military budget goes slightly up or slightly down, these advocates will shout and campaign for what turn out to be minor adjustments in the "right direction."

The only problem is, perhaps half the military budget is there to provide, not defense, but contracts for corporations. Perhaps more.

The whole cold war served as a platform from which hugely expensive R&D could be done by corporations at government/taxpayer expense. This R&D launched the electronics and computers we have today. (So much for free-market capitalism.)

One upper-end estimate of corporate welfare today is 500 billion dollars per year in the US. This would include military contracts and various other subsidies.

3 1

At a Washington press conference on January 21, 1999, Congressman Peter De Fazio pointed out that Bill Clinton is supporting a $100 billion increase over the next five years in the military budget. This astounding gift to corporate America (through military contracts) comes on the heels of a discovered crime.

What is that crime? Have you heard about it? Has Dan Rather been pumping it furiously night after night on the news?

Certainly not.

The federal government's GAO (General Accounting Office) has discovered that the Pentagon cannot account for $43 billion of previous budget monies.

It's missing.

Completely.

Gone.

$43 billion.

The government gave it to the Pentagon and now it's disappeared.

How was it used?

Was it used?

Did it go to Switzerland to float the national budget of a mid-sized nation?

Did it go into corporate hands?

$43 billion.

And the president supports a new increase of $100 billion over the next five years.

3 2

Most people do not realize that before the colonies declared independence from Britain in 1776, the King had set up the entire structure of control in America as companies or crown colonies, as they were called.

The American revolutionaries of the new nation were as suspicious of corporations as they were of kings and state religions. This was reflected in the original structure of corporations in the United States.

State legislatures closely limited—and granted—the charters of all corporations. Any harm to the citizenry and the state legislatures could revoke the charter and immediately put the company out of business.

This was essentially the way the new states were set up.

If this were the case today, most of the biggest transnationals would be out of existence.

But during the 19th century, a corruption in these state laws set in, through bribes of judges by businessmen. Finally, in 1886 the US Supreme Court, in the case of Santa Clara County v. Southern Pacific Railroad, ruled that a corporation was a person, with all the rights of a person. This incredible corruption of earlier law meant that now a corporation could demand due process in court, and could bring to bear, in all actions against it, the full weight of its lawyers and monies and prestige and influence. Until then, the state legislature could simply take a corporation that had done harm and revoke its charter suddenly and throw it out of the state.

In addition to this, corporations now being called persons, could lobby and support candidates for public office.

This led to the overwhelming influence of companies on politics.

33

There are three major types of genetically engineered food now produced by giant corporations.

Produced in growing fields.

1. Seeds inserted with genes that result in only one crop-generation. That is, when a crop grows it drops new seeds, and farmers traditionally pick those up and plant a new crop with them. With this terminator technology, as it's called, that will not be possible. Farmers will have to go back to the corporation which holds patents on the terminator seeds and buy new ones. The corporation becomes Mother Nature.

2. Seeds inserted with genes so that the food-crops that then grow will be able to withstand increased amounts of sprayed herbicides without dying. These so-called herbicide-resistant seeds will tolerate more of THAT CORPORATION'S herbicides. It's that specific.

3. Seeds inserted with bacterial genes that will grow into crops that make their own toxin to kill pests. This is called Bt technology. It brings on victory and survivability and dominance for certain kinds of pests that are resistant to that toxin. This causes its own special brand of problem up the line, especially for organic farms, which are vulnerable to Bt-immune pests.

In no case have studies been done which show that any of these technologies are safe for humans, or safe for the evolutionary future of the planet.

In fact, the fall/winter 1998 issue of *Gene Exchange* (www.ucsvsa.org) indicates that Bt toxins are accumulating in the soil, poisoning it as an ecosystem.

34

In November of 1998, Professor Nanjundaswamy, president of the Kamataka (India) State Farmers Association, issued a statement about experimental Bt cotton fields in Kamataka planted by Monsanto to test genetically engineered seeds:

"Monsanto's [Bt Cotton] field trials in Kamataka will be reduced to ashes in a few days. These actions will start a movement of direct action by farmers against biotechnology, which will not stop until all the corporate killers like Monsanto, Novartis, Pioneer etc. leave the country. We know that stopping biotechnology in India will not be of much help to us if it continues in other countries, [but] if we play our cards right at the global level and coordinate our work, these actions can also pose a major challenge to the survival of these corporations in the stock markets. Who wants to invest in a mountain of ashes, in offices that are constantly being squatted (and if necessary even destroyed) by activists?"

Then on November 28 and December 2, Indian farmers burned those Monsanto cotton fields while TV cameras recorded the event.

Pressure was felt by both the Indian national and provincial governments, because they had secretly collaborated with Monsanto and other agri-transnationals.

On December 3rd, one of the provincial governments, Andhra Pradesh, told Monsanto to stop all their field experiments with genetically engineered cotton seeds in that state.

The Indian national government restated its continuing position that food seeds genetically engineered and patented by Monsanto and, amazingly, by the US Dept. of Agriculture, would not be permitted commercial use in India.

It is generally acknowledged that major chemical companies in America—all of whom would be willing to engineer seeds or are already doing it—have bought up enough food-seed companies in America so that they now corner the market.

There are reports coming out of Korea and Thailand that government officials there are on the road to demanding that any genetic foods in their countries must carry specifying labels. In the US, there are no labels.

In Japan, the national government has been given citizen petitions with several million signatures. These petitions demand the same kind of labeling.

"This food-product has been genetically engineered."

There is a report that US trade officials have told the

Japanese government that mandatory labeling of genetically engineered foods in Japan would lead to a US/Japan trade war.

Again, some of this engineering is for the purpose of allowing the food-crops in the field to withstand the assault of more and more pesticide without curling up and dying—and we eat the pesticide. Some of the genetic engineering is the terminator technology sketched above, or Bt technology. And other engineering is for the purpose of altering the shape or look or shelf-life of the food.

The inserted genes do in fact migrate to other plants in other fields—with unknown results.

In no cases has human testing been done to ensure long-term safety of these technologies. The public is assured by corporations like Monsanto and by government agencies like the FDA that no harm can come from all this, and that therefore labeling foods "genetically engineered" stirs up a false picture of possible danger in consumers' minds.

On December 8th, 1998, 13 environmental organizations staged a mass protest outside Monsanto's corporate offices near Manila. Their slogans were, "Stop the Terminator Seeds" and "Put a Face on the Enemy." Major Philippine newspapers are now covering this issue, and two government officials have introduced a resolution to hold hearings at the national level.

Here is a report from Ronnie Cummins, editor of the excellent journal *Food Bytes* about the current situation in New Zealand. It illustrates significant collusion between corporations selling GE food and the Clinton administration:

"... a major controversy has developed over revelations that a US government official threatened serious government reprisals if the country went forward with a law on mandatory labeling [of all genetically engineered foods in New Zealand]. Former associate Health Minister Neil Kirton revealed in an interview in the national press that the United States

Ambassador, Josiah Beerman, visited him twice in February and March and 'bullied' him over the testing and labeling of genetically modified food. Kirton was later fired and replaced by another government official who was willing to go along with the US 'no labeling' position. Polls in New Zealand and Australia show that consumers overwhelmingly support mandatory labeling. In one 1993 poll in Australia, a full 89% of citizens said they wanted labeling and would reject foods that were unlabeled..."

One of the leading and most credible activists in the battle against genetically engineered crops, Dr. Vandana Shiva, from India, has called Monsanto "a global terrorist" inflicting "hazardous food" on countries around the world.

Mexico and Brazil have also shown opposition to genetically engineered food.

In Mexico City, Green Party members of the national parliament are writing legislation that would require both testing and labeling of gene-altered foods.

In Brazil, Carrefour, a huge chain of supermarkets, has taken a position against the sale of Monsanto's herbicide-resistant soybeans. Brazil ranks number two, globally, in growing soybeans.

A 1998 lawsuit filed by the Brazilian Institute of Consumer Defense put a temporary stop to Brazilian government approval of Monsanto's genetically engineered herbicide-resistant soybeans.

Cummins writes, "At a November international conference of IFOAM (International Federation of Organic Agriculture Movements) at Mar del Plata, Argentina, delegates from more than 60 countries, representing the world's leading organic farming organizations, called for governments and regulatory agencies throughout the world to immediately ban the use of genetic engineering in agriculture and food production because of threats to human health, the environment, and farmers rights."

In Europe, a leak of Monsanto's own sponsored polls showed that "the broad climate is extremely inhospitable to biotechnology acceptance. Over the past year, the situation has deteriorated steadily and is perhaps even accelerating, with the latest survey showing an ongoing collapse of public support for biotechnology and genetically modified (GM) foods."

In October of 1998, all of Austria's supermarket chains said they would refuse to sell genetically engineered foods.

This isn't half of the story.
And yet, where is this in the American press?
Nowhere.
Major network and newspaper editors and reporters know that, when they go to US federal officials or Monsanto officials and ask for the low-down, they get bland assurances that the whole citizen/government resistance business is a tempest in a teacup. They are told that GE foods are safe.

Beyond that, however, there is no doubt that the story in the US is being controlled, stepped on, spiked, covered up.

It is one of the major issues of our time.

And an example of the networks serving masters and committing ultimate suicide.

35

Kings once sent out explorers to find new lands and new wealth and exploit it, for the crown.

In that sense, the monarchy was a corporation.

Spanish rulers profited from the discovery of gold in Latin America.

The crown sold licenses to merchants, and took part of the profit from ventures which involved stealing land and subduing the people who lived on that land.

Yes?

In modern times, we have a partnership of governments

and large corporations. That is the contemporary equivalent of the older situation.

Did only the US government profit from the winning of World War 2?

Did it annex any major lands?

In fact, it appears that the final outcome of the War was to make the economies of the enemies stronger than they had been.

An odd state of affairs.

That would be in line with the thesis that some of the heaviest corporate and political hitters in Germany and the US had, during the War, been partners, been a Fraternity.

This thesis is firmly grounded in Charles Higham's magnificent book, *Trading With the Enemy*. He points out that the very real Fraternity, in the years leading up to World War 2, hoped for a negotiated peace between Germany and the US, which would establish them (the heavy corp and pol leaders) as the de facto rulers of the planet into the future.

A partnership of aspects of governments and corporate and financial figures.

A revolution of insiders, if you will.

A coalescing of greater power among those who already had much power.

From this one would infer that the Fraternity's political leaders (e.g., Allen Dulles) would also make money on the success of joining together big elite players from both sides of the Atlantic. Dulles of course did become head of the CIA. Who knows what other perks and sums and rewards behind the scenes would go to a man like that?

The Fraternity, one would suppose, would be very generous to its own, especially to those who did not shovel in the hugest of the profits, but dedicated themselves in the political arena to greasing the wheels for their corporate brothers.

The big winners from World War 2 were corporate players, the modern equivalent of pirates entering into partnership with their government soulmates.

Corporations who made the weapons and bombs and planes and ships and communication devices.

It's obvious, but we forget that the huge corporations and

their brother governments must act together if either is to be
satisfied.

36

Once upon a time, as Buckminster Fuller has pointed out,
the royals ran the Western world ... but then came technology.

And one of the first technologies was seafaring knowledge.
The great pirates became kings of their own. They knew
where to travel for novel goods, how to get there, and they
could trade and discover secret resources hidden from the
castle-bound rulers.

The royals had run their empires on two myths.

Pure bloodlines uninterrupted through time.

And divine right.

Technology arrived and eroded those myths, and the royals
had to join in a new mixed bag of power.

From that point on there have been many permutations
and combinations, arriving at the modern giant transnational
corporation.

The reason for being a large modern government is ... it
enables its partners: corporations.

37

And of course as we well know, the corporate agenda is
not made on behalf of human beings.

A review of the first 3-4 years of NAFTA, which purport-
edly stands for free trade among companies north and south
of the Mexico border:

The Economic Policy Institute of Washington DC concludes that on balance NAFTA has cost the US 394,835 jobs.

A study by the National Council of La Raza, the William
C Velasquez Institute and UCLA's North American Integra-
tion and Development Center pegs that loss of American jobs
at 91,000.

38

Here are some of the before and after profits of US companies who were involved in World War 1. More than 21,000 new millionaires (or billionaires) were hatched during the War.

- From 1910-1914, Du Pont earned $6 million a year. During the War years, from 1914-1918, Du Pont earned $58 million a year.
- From 1910-1914, Bethlehem Steel made $6 million a year. During the War years? $49 million a year.
- The earnings of US Steel went from $20 million a year to $60 million a year.
- International Nickel Company? From $4 million a year to $73.5 million a year.

This is the way it seems to work, if we boil down the factors:

During the actual time of the War, the US government spent $39 billion.

That money came from taxes paid by citizens, it came from citizens buying Liberty Bonds, and it came from the government printing money.

The profit on the War itself was $16 billion.

Profit? Yes. That is what the 21,000 new millionaires and billionaires took in.

These companies and people who made the great sums were the representatives of the crown, so to speak, and only the most naive would think that key government figures greased the wheels for such profits without getting something themselves.

Bankers during this period played their little cruel game. When huge numbers of Liberty War Bonds had been bought at $100, they depressed the price (after all, why should the price go down unless through intentional manipulation—we were never in danger of losing the War).

They took the price down to $84.

Frightened small investors sold their bonds.

The bankers bought them and then took the price up again

to $100 and beyond. Then they sold and made their gravy.

The soldiers themselves who fought and suffered and died and came home wounded in body and spirit were paid $30 a month during the War.

Of that $30, $15 was automatically subtracted every month to support the soldier's dependents at home. Heaven forbid that the government would offer any support to needy families.

From the remaining $15 in monthly salary the soldier was forced to shell out $6 a month for accident insurance.

Then, finally, soldiers were heavily pressured to buy Liberty Bonds at $100 a crack. All told, they bought $2 billion worth.

So this is the closest accounting you will probably ever see of a war, a major war, reduced to its true and brutal terms.

It is all told in a book by Major General Smedley Butler, a Marine who was there. The book is *War is a Racket*, and in 52 pages it will open your eyes and put a knife in your heart.

39

Woodrow Wilson was elected to a second term as the president in 1916 because he had made a promise to keep the country out of war.

150 days later he told Congress we had to enter and fight the war in Europe.

Well, there had been a meeting.

A sit-down.

A commission from Europe had come to the White House. It represented England, France, Italy. The message? The war was going very badly. Germany was going to win. England, France and Italy already owed US arms manufacturers, bankers, exporters, and other businessmen $6 billion for their "help."

There was no way they could pay that back if they lost the war.

End of debate.

The US was in.

40

In 1937, not long before a new war in Europe, US Ambassador to Germany, William Dodd, sailed to New York. In the harbor, he held a press conference. The *New York Times* printed his remarkable statement:

"A clique of US industrialists is hell-bent to bring a fascist state to supplant our democratic government and is working closely with the fascist regime in Germany and Italy. I have had plenty of opportunity in my post in Berlin to witness how close some of our American ruling class families are to the Nazi regime. On [the ship], a fellow passenger, who is a prominent executive of one of the largest financial corporations [in the US], told me point blank that he would be ready to take definite action to bring fascism into America if President Roosevelt continued his progressive policies."

41

On November 23rd, 1937, there was a very private meeting held in Boston. Attendees? Representatives of General Motors, which was then owned by the Du Pont family. Also Baron Manfred von Killinger, who was running espionage operations for the Nazis on the west coast of the US. Also Baron von Tippleskirsch, leader of private Gestapo operations in Boston.

An agreement was signed among these parties dedicating themselves to the Nazi agenda. There was an understanding that specifically Roosevelt had to be voted out of office, and "Jewish power" in American politics and culture had to be eliminated.

The plan was to bring in a fuhrer to run the United States. The favorite choice was Montana Senator Burton Wheeler.

However, details of this Boston meeting were leaked to journalist George Seldes. He printed an account in his *In Fact* newsletter.

Years later, after the War had begun, Congressman John Coffee, from the state of Washington, placed the whole secret

Boston agreement in the Congressional Record. The date was August 20, 1942. Coffee officially insisted that the Du Ponts and the chiefs of General Motors had to be dealt with.

Nothing was done.

42

The immunity of corporations and their leaders.

A statement from UNICEF:

"One and a half million babies die every year because they are not breastfed. Millions more become ill. What makes a woman believe she cannot breastfeed her baby is the constant undermining of her confidence, by advertising."

Isn't the main culprit Nestle?

We have been taught that corporations are not a subject for study, as if these entities are immune to investigations, as if they exist in a different sphere, protected by the fact that they participate in business, which itself is too mobile and pragmatic and tactical to get a fix on.

Why isn't UNICEF or some front for it suing Nestle, Gerber, Wyeth, Milco and Nutricia?

Nestle, by the way, brings in about $30 billion a year from the sales of its candy, ice cream, pet food, beverages, coffee, tea, wines, cosmetics—and baby food.

43

Dream conversation:

"Let's run an experiment on that planet. Earth."

"Do they have people?"

"They're just beginning to. Pretty dumb."

"What's the experiment?"

"Control. Population control."

"Start with some kind of religion?"

"Best way."

"Then we'll get into science."

"The payoff."

"Show them that healing is possible in certain situations with technology and trained doctors."

"Then cross them up and feed them over a long period of time more and more toxic chemicals. Drugs, agricultural chemicals, empty food, industrial chemicals as pollutants."

"What's the point of the experiment?"

"To see how long they'll go for it. See if we can wipe them out completely before they figure out what's happening."

44

On August 24th, 1994, a watchdog group called Health Action International issued a release indicating that Sandoz, the giant Swiss pharmaceutical corporation (now merged with Ciba-Geigy as Novartis), had just withdrawn one of its drugs from America and Canada.

The drug? Parlodel.

Its strange purpose? To suppress the production of mother's milk in a woman after she gives birth.

The FDA had dragged its heels for five years before stating it was going to withdraw its approval of Parlodel.

During those five years, 531 adverse events had been reported, including 32 deaths. There were other effects from the drug: hypertension, seizure, stroke.

Suddenly the FDA decides that "lactation suppression can be managed effectively—and more safely—by the use of cold packs, compression bandages and pain medication, as needed."

No criminal proceedings against Sandoz or the FDA.

Well of course not, you say.

No. Not of course not.

45

The following item appears in the Fall 1994 issue of *The Compleat Mother:*

"The average caesarean section rate in public hospitals in Brazil is 60%. In private hospitals it is 90%." (Robbie Davis-Floyd, *Dis-Embodied Childbirth*)

46

On October 6, 1933, the president of General Motors, William Knudsen, returned from a trip to Germany. Goring had not taken over General Motors plants there. And for good reason. Knudsen was a member of the Fraternity, and supported the Nazis. Back in New York, Knudsen told reporters that Germany was "the miracle of the twentieth century."

Du Pont owned General Motors.

"Along with friends of the Morgan Bank and General Motors," Charles Higham writes in *Trading with the Enemy*, "certain Du Pont backers financed a coup d'etat that would overthrow the President [Roosevelt] with the aid of a $3 million-funded army of terrorists..."

These businessmen had to find a military leader for the job.

They chose retired Major General and Marine Commandant, recipient of two Congressional Medals of Honor, perhaps the most acclaimed soldier in America, Smedley Butler.

Butler, these businessmen felt, might also take over the country if Roosevelt wouldn't surrender. That would be fine, too.

This plan met with enthusiasm from German leaders like Hermann Schmitz, chairman of IG Farben.

An American lawyer, Gerald MacGuire, was chosen to present the offer to Smedley Butler.

MacGuire visited Butler twice and laid out the plan.

Butler was a critic of Roosevelt and the New Deal, but this was treason.

He played along, expressing interest, and then spoke with President Roosevelt and spilled all the beans.

There was a terrible economic depression in the country at the time. Roosevelt felt he couldn't directly and immediately expose Du Pont and Morgan without causing even greater damage to confidence in "the American way of life."

So Roosevelt had the story leaked to the newspapers, which ran it but spun it at the same time as an unfounded rumor. The leak deflated the planned coup.

Thomas Lamont of Morgan Bank said the idea of such a plot was "Perfect Moonshine!"

A House committee meanwhile investigated. Smedley Butler told the committee to subpoena the Du Ponts, but the committee refused. Ditto for the Morgan Bank.

So Butler told reporters that General Douglas MacArthur was one of the coup plotters.

Articles broke, but no one believed them.

Before the House committee the lawyer MacGuire shrugged off the whole business by saying that Butler had "misunderstood" the conversations they had had.

Four years later, in 1938-39, the committee finally published its conclusions, which were shown to a limited number of people:

"[The] committee was able to verify all the pertinent statements made by General Butler."

The committee report revealed that Remington, a subsidiary of Du Pont, would have been responsible for supplying weapons to an army of a million men, presumably enlisted by General Butler (if he had joined up) from veterans' associations.

No one went to jail.

The whole affair was buried.

47

After World War 2, as the decades wore on, it became more apparent to the new Hermann Schmitzes and Du Ponts and Rockefellers of this world that, although large-scale wars were quite profitable, nationalisms did not have to be acted out on the world stage to produce the conditions under which transnational corporate interests could ascend to even stronger positions.

No, if ties among these corporate gods were made lasting

enough, if store fronts like the International Monetary Fund and the World Bank and the Council on Foreign Relations and the Trilateral Commission and the UN and GATT (and eventually NAFTA) could be created and expanded, then corporations themselves could continue to become the premier island-nations of domination in the world.

These days we are dealing with other kinds of unreported and secret coup d'etats. The promotion of genetically engineered food crops all over the world. The ownership of all the major food-seed companies by chemical corporations which are altering these seeds to absorb more pesticide, or to give birth to only one crop (terminator technology), forcing farmers to come to the corporation every year to buy new seeds.

As I mentioned, the eight largest pesticide companies in the world are Dow, Du Pont, Monsanto, Imperial Chemical Industries (England), Rhone Poulenc (France), Ciba-Geigy (Switzerland, now Novartis after merging with Sandoz), Bayer and Hoechst (Germany).

As cited in, among other sources, the prophetic *Biotechnology's Bitter Harvest*, these companies are all involved in the research and production of genetically engineered food seeds. This research is highly dangerous to the future of the human race, seeing as no human studies have been done or will be done on the long-term effects of planting, growing, and eating various kinds of genetically altered food.

This corporate attitude of invulnerability, or better yet, disinterest in the effects of technology, echoes the attitude of IG Farben, the Nazi cartel. Farben was among the first of the huge world corporations to engage in the mass human testing (on concentration camp inmates) of pharmaceuticals and other toxic chemicals.

One or two sources have indicated that Farben had business ties with most of the above corporations.

In fact, Bayer and Hoechst were two of the three core corporations in the Farben cartel.

Du Pont, whose lifeblood product since its beginnings was gunpowder, formed in 1926 a cartel partnership with Imperial

Chemical Industries (ICI), which itself had just been started by Nobel, the British explosives firm. Du Pont and ICI from that point on shared sales agents all over Latin America and Europe. By 1934, Du Pont and ICI together "owned 20 percent of one of Hitler's munitions makers, DAG, part of the IG Farben combine."

In that same year, Du Pont "had financial and market dealings in war materials or processes with ... Switzerland's CIBA [Geigy], France's Rhone Poulenc..."

A scorecard will not keep track of the players here.

Money and power simply intercede in the game, and ideals and humanity and national geo-names move aside.

48

On September 10, 1934, a US Senate committee convened special hearings on "the munitions issue."

Du Pont, the largest weapons company in America, took center stage.

The committee showed that Du Pont had agreements, before and after World War 1, with German munitions companies. These companies, in which Du Pont owned considerable stock, were now busy arming Hitler.

In that same year, with the Du Ponts emerging from the hearings unscathed, A. Felix du Pont and sister Alice traveled "to the Brazilian plantation of Henry Ford, the Republican Party's strong man. A Nazi sympathizer since 1923, when Hitler personally accorded him special praise, in August 1938 Ford would accept from Hitler the first Grand Cross of the German Eagle ever awarded to an American. This was the man to whom the Du Ponts were drawn in increasing political ties."

49

As of 1984, the Du Ponts controlled assets worth $211 billion.

50

"After Pearl Harbor, the German army, navy, and air force contracted with ITT for the manufacture of switchboards, telephones, alarm gongs, buoys, air raid warning devices, radar equipment, and thirty thousand fuses per month for artillery shells used to kill British and American troops. This was to increase to fifty thousand per month by 1944. In addition, ITT supplied ingredients for the rocket bombs that fell on London, selenium cells for dry rectifiers, high-frequency radio equipment, and fortification and field communication sets.

"Without this supply of crucial materials it would have been impossible for the German air force to kill American and British troops, and for the German army to fight the allies in Africa, Italy, France, and Germany, for England to have been bombed, or for Allied ships to have been attacked at sea...

"Whether or not a trading [with the enemy license] was issued [to ITT by the US government], the trading was continued with the assurance that neither the State Department nor the Department of Justice would intervene."

Do you know a person who served in World War 2, or the family of someone who did?

How long is the statute of limitations on whatever you want to call this—mass murder, treason, depraved indifference?

51

Dream monologue.

"I am a tinpot dictator in the Third World. I am sought after by wealthy foreign men who want to control some of my best lands. This is no problem to me. I can dispossess even more of my people, throw them off their fertile property. I can guarantee these wealthy foreigners that I will keep my subjects in a permanently weakened state through hunger, generation to generation, and the continued contamination of water. I can run sewage directly into the drinking water if necessary. And I do. I have no objection to western doctors and health agencies making my country the target for their pathetic heroic antics. Build a few hospitals, bring in medical drugs. I know what is causing my people to become ill and stay ill, and hospitals and drugs will have no effect on THAT. Wealthy corporate foreigners are willing to pay me very nice sums for the right to use and take pieces of my country. They want to grow coffee and sugar and cocoa and export them to industrialized nations. They want to pay almost no taxes. They want no disturbing revolutions. They want mineral rights. Some of the medical doctors want to be able to call what is killing my weakened subjects AIDS. They can call it anything they want to. The rich foreigners can send toxic and cancer-causing pesticides here and I will let my people use them. Of course. They can also send useless and toxic and unrefrigerated spoiled medical drugs here as well, and I will allow these to be sold out in the open. This is a good partnership. It works on many levels."

52

Contrary to every impulse of the early American citizen, the US federal government has long had the right to "lease public and Indian lands and mineral rights to private corporations. By 1973, the Federal Government had leased 680,854 acres of public and 258,754 acres of Indian land, containing over 20 billion tons of coal, to the corporations. Leasing halted in 1973 and did not begin again until late spring of 1979, because there was criticism of the fact that 70% of the land leased was going to only 15 multinational oil companies— Shell, Sun, ARCO, Gulf, Exxon, Mobil, etc."

Compare that with this situation abroad—after the US Marines spent much of the first half of the 20th century occupying Nicaragua and overseeing it, Franklin Roosevelt appointed the Somoza family to take over the country and look after US interests in the region. The Somozas were then backed by every US president until their overthrow in 1979. The Somoza family ran the CONDECA military forces which joined with banana companies to make sure US corporations were secure throughout Central America.

The Somozas in Nicaragua owned 1 out of every 10 square feet of arable land.

This was an absolute tyranny. State-sponsored terrorism was used all the way along the line to keep the population in tow and obedient.

53

Genetically engineered seeds now grow on 51 million acres in the US.

No tests show that the crops of these seeds are safe, long-term, to eat. And as the genes come back generation after generation in the crops, what will happen? What will happen as the genes drift into other crops?

These food seeds are patented by companies.

Corporations owning life.

That is the ultimate end-game.

Monsanto has contracted with a number of investigators to follow up leads on seed thieves.

These would be farmers who decided to take the falling seeds from the crops which themselves originally came from genetically engineered seeds. Second generation GE seeds.

Plant them again.

But no.

This is illegal.

You can't watch a GE crop grow and then scoop up the seeds that drop and replant them.

No.

Against the law.

Monsanto has filed 475 seed-theft cases across the US.

250 of these are being pursued.

100 have already been settled.

One settled case is instructive.

David Chancy, a Kentucky farmer, admitted that he scooped up drop-off GE seeds from his GE soybean crop and "illegally traded the pirated seed with neighbors..."

So Chancy must now pay $35,000 in royalties to Monsanto. Chancy will keep his soybean farm records open to Monsanto for inspection over the next five years.

Monsanto has made other farmers destroy their crops.

This sounds like a perverse Sunday school story, only the teacher has a gun and courts and judges to back him up.

And patents which say he owns little pieces of life.

54

The International Monetary Fund (IMF) draws its monies from nations around the world. With loans, it then bails out countries which are economically on the ropes. However, "The IMF can use its leverage over cash-strapped developing countries to force them to open up their economies to powerful Northern multinational corporations, even before a country has built up its domestic economy."

This is a key point.

This is a very key point.

The recent crash of several Asian economies was, to a degree, based on a fast in-and-out of foreign investors to the tune of $110 billion in one year.

This was more than Thailand, Indonesia, the Philippines, and Malaysia could take.

The IMF is at the service of giant corporations, at the expense of ... everything else.

55

Dream conversation:

IMF: "Corcovado is about to default on its international debt. A small vulnerable country."

Mystery CEO: "Lots of lumber there."

IMF: "Indeed."

MCEO: "We'd certainly be interested in investing there. Cutting down trees is our life, and exporting the raw timber. But not at the wages they're paying laborers now. And their environmental regulations would kill us."

IMF: "Funny coincidence. Those concerns would be solved by the conditions of our bailout there."

MCEO: "Really?"

IMF: "Yes. Knocks me out. You see, we lend Corcovado a few billion, on the condition that they slash government spending. So the first agencies to go, usually, are social welfare and the environment. That means their government will only have a tenuous connection to medical benefits for workers, environmental rules, and even wages. Everything is privatized. The government basically just stands by and watches corporations like you come in and rape and pillage and export the results."

MCEO: "Nine cents an hour and lots of dioxin in the rivers."

IMF: "It would go unnoticed."

MCEO: "By the way, I assume that part of the social programs of the government that would be cut involve feeding people."

IMF: "Absolutely."

MCEO: "Well, when we come into a country like this, we have that effect too. You know, we throw people off the land they've had in the family for generations. We dispossess thousands and thousands of people."

IMF: "So?"

MCEO: "Hunger is a good weakener of the dispossessed person. We need that. Keeps him from organizing and revolting. But we may need additional help to keep the indigenous people in line."

IMF: "You mean military?"

MCEO: "And the action wing of intelligence agencies."

IMF: "We're a peace-loving agency. We leave all that up to you."

MCEO: "Whatever it takes."

IMF: "Of course, we don't want to hurt anybody."

MCEO: "Neither do we."

IMF: "By the way, we see that another big company is itching to move into Corcovado."

MCEO: "Really? Who is that?"

IMF: "Can't really say, but they're agri. They grow genetically engineered food."

MCEO: "Oh, I know who you mean. We have a few of their people on our board. And some of the same Washington connections."

IMF: "Of course there have never been any human tests on genetically engineered food."

MCEO: "No problem. The marketing of the food is the test. All life is an experiment, in a way."

IMF: "Critics say the implanted genes drift into other plants. So that could be affecting evolution in ways we don't understand. And eating the genes may have unforseen health effects too. If our food undergoes a subtle change, we may not get the nutrition we need from it. That would create illness on a vast scale."

MCEO: "Evolution is what we make it. Who knows? In a hundred years, the makeup of this planet could be quite different."

IMF: "What do you mean?"

MCEO: "Survival of the fittest. That floats all boats worth floating. It answers all doubts."

IMF: "Why the hell not?"

56

There has been much talk about the meaning of the international GATT (General Agreement on Tariffs and Trade).

This agreement and organization is built to serve corporations, and you can basically read "corporations" for "nations."

Through concepts like "harmonization" and "free trade" (a complete misnomer) certain traditions will be scrapped. Health and safety laws in individual nations will be destroyed over time, over the long haul, so that corporations worry less and less about shipping toxic: pesticides, GE foods, chemicals, building materials, and pharmaceuticals from nation to nation. So that nations which demand that foreign businesses within their shores must have a 51% local partner will be converted on a tide of "goodwill" about doing business without hindrances. Nations themselves will take more and more of a back seat to the collections of corporations elevated by GATT.

The World Trade Organization (WTO), which is the enforcement arm of GATT, will ensure—unless derailed—that GE food cannot be refused by any nation, that every nation must import GE food, because "scientifically" there is no objection to it.

If such a judgement is made and backed up, it will be the ultimate victory for fake corporate science, because of course there ARE very serious rational objections to allowing the domestic growing or the importing of GE food.

Such transcendental fake science will also allow international "free trade" in toxic industrial chemicals, toxic pesticides, and toxic and unworkable pharmaceuticals—all under the name of "these products have been proved to be safe and effective."

This is the strategy, this is the road the corporations have built.

57

1995. General Sani Abacha, the dictator of Nigeria, executes nine human rights activists, including Ken Saro-Wiwa.

"Washington rang with calls for tough action against ... Abacha."

Clinton backed off, just as he backed off in China.

Why?

US oil companies are firmly entrenched in Nigeria. Mobil, Amoco, Chevron. Mobil puts together a report which announces that "US companies have a substantial and long-term interest in the stability" of Nigeria.

Translation. If human rights gain a foothold over and against tyranny, it would be bad for business. Abacha might kick out the US companies. Or a new ruler who really cared about his people might suddenly change labor laws and environmental laws in Nigeria and lessen corporate profits.

58

May 28, 1998.

Nigerian protestors take over the Chevron oil platform in the Niger Delta. They want Chevron to "contribute more to the development of the impoverished oil region where they live."

Chevron helps the government's kill-and-go Mobile Police by transporting them by helicopter, at government request, to the platform.

Violence breaks out.

The Police kill two Nigerian activists and wound others.

Oh yes. Governments usually do well when they let multinationals operate in their countries free and unhindered. In this case, "The [Nigerian] government owns 60 percent of the oil operation, while Chevron holds a 40 percent stake." But the people of Nigeria don't see much of that 60 percent.

59

In July 1997, the World Health Organization published papers on asbestos and safety which shocked several experts. These papers sounded like they had been written by representatives of asbestos companies.

Asbestos? Cancer? No problem.

The kicker is this. The World Trade Organization (WTO), the operating arm of the global "free trade agreement" called GATT, can consult this junk science on asbestos and use it to force countries—like France—who have completely banned the use of asbestos, to knuckle under.

Canada, a major producer of asbestos, plans to challenge France's ban as an unfair trade practice. That means Canada, before the WTO in Geneva, will argue that recent studies reveal asbestos to be safe. If the WTO agrees, France's position is overridden. If France then refuses to import asbestos from Canada ("violating free trade") they would be forced to pay annual gigantic fines or face serious international trade sanctions, in which member nations of GATT would boycott commerce with them.

This is one way in which GATT was formulated to serve corporations over and against safety as defined by nations. GATT was yet another cornerstone in building a global economy run by and for the transnationals.

At the time of its passage by the US, GATT was debated by the Congress with barely a mention of the overriding corporate essence involved.

The entire Congress is not that stupid.

60

Synthesize. Fabricate.

That is the modern imperative emerging from large tyrannies.

Introduce fake science whenever necessary and dress it up with the convincing imprimatur of established authority.

Of course one corporate concern around the world is violence stemming from severe hunger and poverty. Whether some corporation in a given area was a primary cause of bringing on those conditions, or simply took advantage of them to dominate a nation, the corps worry is that business as usual could be disrupted.

So "solve" violence.

Governments, by and large, agree.

Solve rebellion against injustice.

Good for business, good for government.

In that light:

Boston. Early 1970s.

The Boston Violence Center.

Two neurosurgeons: Vernon Mark and William Sweet.

And a psychiatrist, a former student of Robert Heath,

Frank Ervin. Heath, at Tulane University, was famous for sticking electrodes into people's brains and measuring reactions.

Sweet told the New York state legislature that a brain disease he called psychomotor epilepsy was the cause of violence in American inner cities during the riots and protests of the 60s.

Three years later, Sweet, Mark, and Ervin obtained $500,000 from the National Institute of Mental Health, plus an attached grant from the US Justice Department. Until public exposure cancelled the grant monies, these three doctors were planning to look for areas of the brain that could be surgically removed to prevent ANY violent behavior.

In the early 70s, Louis West of the UCLA Neuropsychiatric Institute tried to obtain a million-dollar grant from the state of California and the US Law Enforcement Assistance Administration. He would establish, north of LA, a Center for the Study and Reduction of Violence. West was interested in mind-altering drugs, brain surgery and chemical castration (cyproterone acetate) as potential cures for violent behavior. The target for testing? Inner-city youth, mostly black and Latino. West was also discussing the implantation of homing receivers in the brain.

The whole West proposal was publicly exposed and the funds were cancelled in 1974.

On February 11, 1992, Frederick Goodwin, the highest-ranking psychiatrist in the federal government, head of the US Alcohol, Drug Abuse, and Mental Health Administration, gave a speech to the National Health Advisory Council on his National Violence Initiative.

He compared inner city youth to monkeys and the inner city itself he characterized as a jungle. ("If you look, for example, at male monkeys, especially in the wild, roughly half of them survive to adulthood. The other half die by violence ... Now, one could say that ... maybe it isn't just the careless use of the word when people call certain areas of certain cities jungles...")

He advocated a program—which he said would be the prime priority for funding in 1994 for the National Institute of Mental Health. Medical personnel would go into inner city schools and measure children for biological markers predictive of future violent behavior.

Never mind that such markers have never been found.

Goodwin was mainly implying that levels of a neurotransmitter in the brain called serotonin were very significant. Too little serotonin and more crime.

This hypothesis has never been proven.

However, there are drugs, such as Prozac, which have the capacity to raise levels of serotonin.

So ... test young children and give them Prozac and other similar drugs. Toxic drugs which have garnered public reports of suicidal and murderous behavior.

Once again, public exposure has put this program on the shelf. But the pressure for this madness doesn't stop.

61

Let me ask a simple question.

Why is it that certain drugs cause the symptoms they are supposed to cure?

Why can chemotherapy be carcinogenic?

Why does AZT attack the bone marrow, where certain cells of the immune system are manufactured, for a condition, AIDS, whose hallmark is supposed to be immune suppression?

Why are the neuroleptic drugs able to create brain damage as they "treat," for example, schizoid conditions in which the brain is said to be already impaired?

And why would any sane person suggest the possibility of (1) diagnosing children as "violence-prone" and then (2) giving them drugs which have brought on violent behavior in people?

Consider the *Physician's Desk Reference* (*PDR*) statement on the Marion Merrell Dow antidepressant called Norpramin: "It is important that this drug be dispensed in the least possible quantities [whatever that might be in a specific case] to depressed outpatients since suicide has been accomplished with this class of drug."

Some of the effects reported from Norpramin are: both elevating and lowering blood sugar levels, heart block, myocardial infarction, stroke, hallucinations, delusions, tremors, ataxia, peripheral neuropathy, seizures, dilation of urinary tract, bone marrow depression, vomiting, black tongue, hepatitis, impotence, painful ejaculation, testicular swelling, weight gain or loss.

Does it occur to you that the addition of any one of these "side-effects" might cause an already depressed person to go over the edge and commit suicide?

Ritalin, the Ciba-Geigy speed-drug prescribed for over a million children in the US—for a mixed-bag "condition" called Attention Deficit Disorder—is said to have a paradoxical effect among the young. That is, although it causes hyperactivity among adults, for already hyperactive children it has a calming action.

The truth is, long-term use of this drug by children can bring back the hyperactivity in spades, along with other symptoms that are simply the results of speed use of any kind. Insomnia, rage, confusion, despair.

Diethylstilbestrol, an Eli Lilly drug, is a synthetic estrogenic substance used for breast cancer and prostate cancer as a palliative (despite the disastrous effects of its prior history with pregnant mothers).

The *PDR* states, under the heading of this drug, in bold letters, "WARNING: USE OF ESTROGENS HAS BEEN REPORTED TO INCREASE THE RISK OF ENDOMETRIAL CARCINOMA..."

Additionally, the January 28, 1994 *Congressional Quarterly* in its report, "Regulating Pesticides," points out that pollutants in the environment are being found to contain estrogenic substances. And several researchers have linked exposure to estrogens with cancer, including breast cancer.

Yet, incredibly, diethylstilbestrol is used as a palliative treatment for breast cancer.

The Du Pont Pharma Company makes a drug called Revia, which is used to treat alcohol dependence. Nevertheless, the *PDR* states, "Its use in patients with active liver disease must be carefully considered in light of its hepatoxic effects ...

Patients should be warned of the risk of hepatic injury and advised to stop the use of Revia and seek medical attention if they experience symptoms of acute hepatitis."

Let's see.

Alcoholism.

Liver disease?

Sure. Isn't that often a side-effect?

So we'll use a drug to treat that person which is very toxic to the liver.

Good idea.

Excellent idea.

And while we're at it, let's use that drug which can bring on breast cancer to treat breast cancer.

Sure. Why not?

And the drug that mangles the bone marrow and creates immune suppression?

Don't tell me. Let me guess. We'll use it for AIDS.

Right. And the antidepressant that poses a risk of suicide?

For depressed people who are thinking about suicide.

Exactly.

I see.

62

This has another spinoff.

The promotion of a myth that destruction caused by a chemical (or toxin) is really being caused by a germ.

The germ, of course, must be treated with other chemicals.

This was the case with the condition called SMON in Japan I described earlier.

When people began to go blind and die and develop various nerve problems, this was called a disease, and the best of the Japanese medical establishment went after the problem—in order to find the germ that was causing the disease.

It was only because of a courageous lawyer and certain medical rebels that the attention was pulled to a drug, clioquinol, and a corporation that made that drug, Ciba-Geigy.

The chemical and company were the cause of SMON.

When a drug is given for symptoms, and the drug causes some of those symptoms, then overwhelmingly the physician tells the patient that he is simply suffering from the disease for which he is being treated. It's a bind.

I know of cases in which perfectly healthy men were diagnosed as HIV positive, given AZT immediately, and then developed symptoms of "AIDS." They went to their doctors, who told them they were just at a more advanced stage of HIV disease. Some believed this, continued to take AZT, and died.

Politically, a chemical is not as good as a germ—if a government or other group is in the business of causing terror and destruction of human life. First of all, with a chemical—like a pesticide which is causing nerve afflictions—when you publicly discover that it is the problem, a corporation will suffer instead of the victims. Furthermore, no doctor, as a cover, will be able to come on the scene and talk about disease and germs and med drugs. The cure for a chemical is to stop spreading the chemical and to prosecute the perpetrator.

Let us suppose that someone designs a terrorizing outbreak of "disease" which will suddenly overwhelm a community. It will make national news. Doctors will be brought in as ultimate authorities. We will have curfews and quarantines, and people will not be allowed to assemble, for fear of contagion.

The perfect repressive event, staged as a biological tragedy.

Human rights can be stripped away in a second, under the cover of medical necessity.

The worshipped almighty doctor gets to play the hero, as he tells Dan Rather about death tolls and makeshift hospital tents and researchers bravely working around the clock to come up with a vaccine.

But there is no germ. There is no disease.

A chemical was let loose and it is poisoning people.

The chemical has a limited range. It runs its course.

In the case of a germ, the results are much more iffy. People with strong immune systems often don't get sick at all. The sci-fi idea that germ-perpetrators have an antidote (vaccine) ahead of time is a myth. Immunization is famous for failing to work, and for causing the very condition it is supposed to prevent. The literature is full of such situations.

No—a chemical hiding behind the cover story about a germ is much more convincing.

63

Updated figures from the consumer organization, The Pure Food Campaign (www.purefood.org):

Presently there are 51.3 million acres in the US planted with genetically engineered crops.

In the world? 69.5 million acres.

In the US there are 34 different commercial crops that are genetically engineered.

500,000 to 600,000 cows are being injected every week in the US with the genetically engineered BGH (bovine growth hormone).

Virtually every processed food in the supermarket that is not organic and contains corn or soy has at least traces of genetically engineered corn or soy.

How can I tell what is what? the consumer wails.

You can't in 99.9999 percent of the cases, because, despite all sorts of federal rules about mandatory labeling of foods, the genetically engineered label is not mandatory.

At the moment, because of heavy insistence from the private community of organic growers and consumers, the "organic" label on food still means among other things that the food is not genetically engineered.

64

As of December 1998, the following genetically engineered crops have been approved by the US government for commercial use:

Four versions of canola, radicchio, 12 versions of corn, 5 versions of cotton, papaya, 2 versions of potato, 3 versions of soybean, 2 versions of squash, 5 versions of tomato.

Then there are five genetically engineered microorganisms which have been approved for use as insect pest control in crop fields.

65

Here is a 1998 statement from Val Giddings, vice president of the Biotechnology Industry Organization, the trade group for biotech companies:

"Within five years—and certainly within 10—some 90-95% of plant-derived food material in the United States will come from genetically engineered techniques [which means that these complexes of altered natural plant materials will be OWNED by corporations]. It'll take a little bit longer for these technologies to penetrate into the organic market, but it will."

66

December 10, 1998.

A press release from NORML, the National Organization to Reform Marijuana Laws.

"Legislation approved by Congress last month allocates $23 million toward developing a new [genetically engineered] fungus aimed at destroying drug-producing plants like marijuana...

"Professor Paul Arriola, an expert in plant genetics at Elmhurst College in Illinois [stated], "It's frightening to think that in the search for a quick fix, we might cause ourselves more long-term ecological and social problems..."

Like the genes that drift out of the plants in which they've been inserted, the fungus moves this way and that across the land.

Coming to your home.

67

An astonishing journal paper.
November, 1993.
FASEB Journal, volume 7, pp.1381-1385.
Authors—Stephan Dirnhofer et al. Dirnhofer is from the Institute for Biomedical Aging Research of the Austrian Academy of Sciences.

A quote from the paper: "Our study provides insights into possible modes of action of the birth control vaccine promoted by the Task Force on Birth Control Vaccines of the WHO (World Health Organization)."

A birth control vaccine?
What?
Yes.
A vaccine whose purpose is to achieve non-pregnancy where it ordinarily could occur.
Sterilization?
This particular vaccine is apparently just one of several anti-fertility vaccines the Task Force is promoting.
Yes. There is a Task Force on Birth Control Vaccines at WHO.
This journal paper focuses on a hormone called human chorionic gonadotropin B (hCG).
There is a heading in the paper (p.1382) called "Ability of antibodies to neutralize the biological activity of hCG."
The authors are trying to discover whether a state of no-fertility can be achieved by blocking the normal activity of hCG.
They state, "We conclude from our results that both the efficacy and safety of the WHO vaccine are not yet ensured."

68

Another journal paper.
The British Medical Bulletin, volume 49, 1993.
"Contraceptive Vaccines" is the title of the paper.
The authors—RJ Aitken et al. From the MRC Reproductive

Biology Unit, University of Edinburgh, Edinburgh, UK.

"Three major approaches to contraceptive vaccine development are being pursued at the present time. The most advanced approach, which has already reached the stage of phase 2 clinical trials [human trials testing efficacy], involves the induction of immunity against human chorionic gonadotrophin (hCG). Vaccines are being engineered ... incorporating tetanus or diptheria toxoid linked to a variety of hCG-based peptides ... Clinical trials have revealed that such preparations are capable of stimulating the production of anti-hCG antibodies. However, the long-term consequences of such immunity in terms of safety or efficacy are, as yet, unknown..."

The authors are talking about creating an immune response against a female hormone.

Training a woman's body to react against one of its own secreted hormones.

The authors state, "The fundamental principle behind this approach to contraceptive vaccine development is to prevent the maternal recognition of pregnancy by inducing a state of immunity against hGC, the hormone that signals the presence of the embryo to the maternal endocrine system."

Very clear.

Stop the female body from recognizing a state of pregnancy. Get the body to treat the natural hormone hCG as an intruder, a disease agent, and mobilize the forces of the immune system against it.

Create a synthetic effect, an engineered effect, by which the mother's "maternal endocrine system" does not swing into gear when pregnancy occurs. The result? The embryo in the mother is swept away by her next period—since hGC, which signals the existence of the pregnancy and halts menstruation cycles, is now treated as a disease entity.

The authors put it this way: "In principle, the induction of immunity against hGC should lead to a sequence of normal, or slightly extended, menstrual cycles during which any pregnancies would be terminated..."

Miscarriage would then be the "normal" state of affairs.

These authors leave no doubt about who the target of this vaccine would be. They do not discuss women in Boston or

Los Angeles. They do not talk about a woman here or there in America who wants to prevent pregnancy over the long term.

The authors begin this paper with these words: "During the next decade the world's population is set to rise by around 500 million. Moreover, because the rates of population growth in the developing countries of Africa, South America, and Asia will be so much greater than the rest of the world, the distribution of this dramatic population growth will be uneven..."

Two other vaccine methods are described. They "aim to prevent conception by interfering with the intricate cascade of interactive events that characterize the union of male and female gametes at fertilization."

There is one other point. Why is the hCG component of the contraceptive vaccine linked, as the authors say, to tetanus or diptheria toxoid? Those are two vaccines already in use. Apparently they function as necessary and indispensable carriers of the hCG component, so that the body will be fooled into making antibodies against, say, both the tetanus and the hCG.

But of course the diptheria and tetanus would also function as a social and political mask—to hide the sterilizing intent as millions of women in the Third World receive vaccines they are told will protect them against infections and disease.

69

A letter to a medical journal.
The Lancet. p.1222. Volume 339. May 16, 1992.
"Cameroon: Vaccination and politics."

Peter Ndumbe and Emmanuel Yenshu, the authors of this letter, report on their efforts to analyze widespread popular resistance to a tetanus vaccine given in the northwest province of Cameroon.

Two of the reasons people rejected the vaccine: it was given only to "females of childbearing age," and people heard that a "sterilizing agent" was present in the vaccine.

70

Well-known journalist Alexander Cockburn, on the op ed page of the *LA Times* on September 8, 1994, reviews the infamous Kissinger-commissioned 1974 National Security Study Memorandum 200, "which addressed population issues."

"... the true concern of Kissinger analysts [in Memorandum 200] was maintenance of US access to Third World resources. They worried that the 'political consequences' of population growth [in the Third World] could produce internal instability ... With famine and food riots and the breakdown of social order in such countries, [the Kinssinger memo warns that] 'the smooth flow of needed materials will be jeopardized.'"

In other words, too many people equals disruption for the transnational corporations who have stolen nations from those very people.

Cockburn notes that the writers of the Kissinger memo "favored sterilization over food aid."

He goes on to say that "By 1977, Reimart Ravenholt, the director of AID's [US Agency for International Development] population program, was saying that his agency's goal was to sterilize one-quarter of the world's women."

71

I have not confirmed reports from the Philippines and Mexico that their 1993 tetanus vaccination programs—which were supposedly administered only to women of childbearing age—involved multiple injections.

Tetanus vaccine protocols indicate that one injection is good for ten years.

Therefore, multiple injections would indicate another motive for the vaccinations—such as the anti-fertility effect of hCG planted in the vaccine.

Inquiries to Philippine officials have gone unanswered.

The organization Population Research Institute (www.pop.org), in the November/December 1996 issue of its *Review*, published a report by David Morrison.

Morrison states, "Philippine women may have been un-wittingly vaccinated against their own children, a recent study conducted by the Philippine Medical Association (PMA) has indicated.

"The study tested random samples of a tetanus vaccine for the presence of human chorionic gonadotropin (hCG), a hormone essential to the establishment and maintenance of pregnancy ... The PMA's positive test results indicate that just such an abortifacient may have been administered to Philippine women [how many?] without their consent.

"The PMA notified the Philippine Department of Health (PDOH) of these findings in a 16 September letter signed by the researchers and certified by its President. Using an im-munological assay developed by the Food and Drug Admin-istration in the United States, a three-doctor research panel tested forty-seven vials of tetanus vaccine collected at random from various health centers in Luzon and Mindanao. Nine were found to contain hCG in levels ranging from 0.191680 mIU/ml to 3.046061 mIU/ml. These vaccines, most of which were labeled as of Canadian origin, were supplied by the World Health Organization as part of a WHO-sponsored vaccination program."

Morrison's article would seem to indicate that the vials of vaccine tested came from a widespread immunization cam-paign rather than from a small pilot study of a few women

So far, I have not been able to get a copy of this letter sent by the PMA to the Philippine Dept. of Health.

72

Stan Freni is a researcher who, in 1994, wrote a paper about fluorides, the substances in many toothpastes also pumped intentionally into the drinking water of many communities and cities.

America had been told many times, over decades, that anyone who thought fluorides were dangerous was a right-wing nut with delusions about "the purity of bodily fluids."

That was a very successful PR campaign.

Funny thing is, Stan Freni wrote his paper as an employee for the US Food and Drug Administration (FDA).

The title of the paper is "Exposure to High Fluoride Concentrations in Drinking Water is Associated With Decreased Birth Rates."

It was published in the *Journal of Toxicology and Environmental Health* (v.42, pp.109-121, 1994).

Freni writes, "A US database of drinking water systems was used to identify index counties with water systems reporting fluoride levels of at least 3ppm (parts per million)."

"... the annual total fertility rate (TFR) for women in the age range 10-49 yr. was calculated for the period 1970-1988," Freni continues.

He concludes, "Most regions showed an association of decreasing TFR with increasing fluoride levels."

73

The FDA approves genetically engineered food for sale. Its policy is to allow food, with few exceptions, into the market WITH NO LABELS, NO IDENTIFICATION. Then if complaints ensue and people drop like flies, it will consider a recall.

This means that the FDA relies on the companies which engineer the food to succeed in making safe foods.

74

The soybeans, corn, canola, papaya, potatoes, tomatoes, squash, radicchio, and dairy products which are GE are "spliced with genes of bacteria or viruses."

Genes from soil bacteria are used to produce the Bt toxin. These genes are implanted in crops which then make their own Bt toxin to kill pests.

Some foods also contain genes from a rabies vaccine.

75

"The following products may also be genetically altered or originate from genetically engineered organisms: enzymes used in the processing of cheese, candies, cookies, breads, cereals, corn syrups, oils, juices, detergents, dough conditioners, yeast, sugar, animal feed and vitamins."

76

Putting genes into plants is not an exact science, in terms of where the gene is finally located every time or what the long-term effects will be. New proteins could be produced that are toxic, for example. The plant could mutate over time and become something else.

77

Roundup Ready soy is a patented name. A Monsanto property, it indicates soy beans which have been GEed to tolerate the Monsanto herbicide, Roundup.

The theory is, we will make a soybean which doesn't fall down in the fields and die when we spray higher levels of Roundup on it. The higher levels of Roundup kill the weeds and that's good.

However, in tests that have been done on the similar Vica faba bean, and on cows who eat GE soy, there is an indication that the GE soy reacts to the Roundup by developing more estrogenic substances within itself. Much has been written about the possible health effects of estrogenic materials. See earlier section on diethylstilbestrol and the accompanying warning about estrogens in the *PDR*.

78

Alfalfa, apple, broccoli, corn, rice, tobacco, walnut, grapes et al have been GEed with genes from the Bt bacterium.

This means these crops will produce their own pesticide, their own toxin, which will kill pests.

But one problem is: these GEed plants will allow super-survival for pests that are naturally resistant to Bt and THOSE pests will thrive and take over the scene.

Bt—not the genes—but the bacterium itself is used as a natural pesticide in organic farming, the only kind of farming that currently guarantees that GE is not used.

So here is a very possible outcome.

The GE crops which contain Bt genes allow the rise of huge numbers of thriving pests which are resistant to Bt, and those pests then attack the organic crops in such numbers that organic farming is dealt a crippling blow.

79

A year or two ago, a website on The Great Boycott, a boycott against the eight largest pesticide companies in the world, received a note from a representative of Monsanto. He said we were saying Roundup was a bad thing, but in truth it breaks down into harmless elements. (I had started The Great Boycott in early 1996.)

I have now discovered a reference I would point this gentleman to. It occurs on page 49 of the excellent, compressed book, *Genetically Engineered Foods* (see end notes). The reference mentions that *The Manchester Guardian*, the well-known British newspaper, on December 15, 1997, reported that "the New York attorney general's office forced Monsanto to withdraw advertisements claiming that Roundup is biodegradable and environmentally friendly. According to the school of health at the University of California, glyphosphate [the active ingredient of Roundup] is the third most commonly reported cause of pesticide illness among farm workers."

80

Dream conversation.

"Let's go to Chile. We'll take the corporate jet."

"Why?"

"I hear they have an ancient grain that no one has discovered."

"Yeah?"

"We bring back samples and patent it."

"We can do that?"

"Sure. The political climate is good for it. A few people did it with a type of quinoa grain in '94."

"The Clinton administration loves GE food."

"If we patent this grain from Chile in the US, and a company in Chile decides to export it here, we might be able to deny it entry with our patent, unless they pay us a royalty."

"It looks pretty good for us. As time goes by, better and better."

"Own the world."

"Every bacteria, butterfly and lion."

81

AIDS is a perfect cover story, a smokescreen behind which depopulation events and strategies can be staged.

"Well, they all got AIDS and died. It was HIV. Nothing could be done."

I will not argue the complete case on AIDS here; I have done that in my 1988 book AIDS INC., which shows why HIV has never been proved to cause any disease, why the HIV test is a very wide net that catches all sorts of irrelevant body-conditions and falsely registers them as HIV-positive, and why AIDS is not an It but a collection of various kinds of devastating immune-suppressing conditions around the world. Caused by multiple factors.

That said, in the coming century, we may see HIV used in an accelerated way as a cover for depopulation in the Third World.

It is in fact already being used, steadily, as a cover for the generation to generation hunger and dirty water that plague Africa, that bring on various infections and widespread death.

82

Third World countries are viewed by elites as "colonies." It is understood that the indigenous people are very angry at the incursion and corporate takeover of their lands.

Depopulation is considered a "strategy" that would keep the disruption of revolutions to a minimum in those places— and keep open corporate access to land and strategic minerals.

83

Too many people in this world, about 4 billion, cannot afford the products of massive companies.

Multinationals sometimes think:

Our whole future lies in China.

In which case, anything would justify the effort to open up that nation as a consumer base.

In addition, certain elites—echoing Nazi plans—could be thinking:

"We must eventually wipe off the map a number of 'Third World peoples' and repopulate those fertile lands with people who are primed and prepared and programmed and indoctrinated to join our global marketplace and become good citizens of the good life as we define it."

84

Let us suppose that there is another force somewhat apart from the transnational corporations, and that is an aristocracy which is not particularly enamored of the global marketplace and "the gross cheapness" it implies. This breed wants very few people, perhaps under a billion on the face of the Earth.

This breed wants ecology in pristine form.

This breed might want, say, automation underground to provide all the blessings of technology.

No smoke, no noise, few people.

Just gentility, and the modulated presence of artisans who, at the bottom of the hill, down from the estate, produce lovely things for the ruling class.

When a liver transplant would be needed by one of the ruling class, the doctors would go to a file drawer in a freezer lab, and they would remove a brand new liver which had been cloned years earlier from that person's own flesh, and they would implant it.

This group of aristocrats would be very interested in de-population, and they would be happy to sweep a number of loud corporations off the map too.

85

The following statement is from *Global Dreams*:

"Over the past two decades images of consumption have been transmitted across the planet, but for most of the world the dreams are unrealizable for both economic and psychological reasons. About two-thirds of the people on earth cannot connect most of the glamorous products they see on billboards and on television with their own lives of poverty and struggle. The expanding cornucopia of globally distributed goods is largely irrelevant to the basic needs of most people in the world.

"New islands of affluence—in China and in a few other countries—are appearing on the horizon, but whether these enclaves are big enough to absorb the already huge but expanding global capacity for producing goods and services is dubious."

Another summing up of the current paradigm by Barnet and Cavanaugh in *Global Dreams*:

"The surplus of gifted, skilled, undervalued, and unwanted

human beings is the Achilles heel of this emerging global [economic] system. The problem is starkly simple: An astonishingly large and increasing number of people are not needed or wanted to make the goods or to provide the services that the paying customers of the world can afford. The gathering pressures of global competition to cut costs [by laying off huge numbers of workers] threaten the vast majority of the 8 billion human beings expected to be living on earth in the first quarter of the next century with the prospect that they will be neither producers or consumers."

86

(See *Biotechnology and Development Monitor*, No. 25, December 1995, Amsterdam, The Netherlands, p.1, "The Development of Anti-Fertility Vaccines, Challenging the Immune System," by Ute Sprenger.)

In 1989, the World Health Organization held a symposium on its anti-fertility vaccine programs. The chairman gave his overview:

"Foremost in my mind during these discussions was our difficulty in assessing the urgency of the demographic crisis. To the extent that the impact of that crisis increases, the need for more effective family planning technologies must increase. At the very least, failure to develop something that may provide a more effective technology would be to take a grave and unnecessary risk."

Of course by 'demographic' he meant the distribution of population globally.

87

The Task Force on Vaccines for Fertility Regulation was created at WHO in 1973.

Ute Sprenger, writing in *Biotechnology and Development Monitor* (December 1995) describes this Task Force as a "global coordinating body for anti-fertility vaccine R&D ... such as anti-sperm and anti-ovum vaccines and vaccines designed to neutralize the biological functions of hCG."

Sprenger indicates that, globally, as of 1995, there were 5 large and many small groups researching these vaccines.

1. WHO/HRP. HRP is the Special Programme of Research, Development and Research Training in Human Reproduction. WHO/HRP is located in Switzerland. It is funded by "the governments of Sweden, United Kingdom, Norway, Denmark, Germany and Canada, as well as the UNFPA and the World Bank."

2. The Population Council is a US group funded by "the Rockefeller Foundation, the National Institutes of Health [a US government agency, the largest single medical research facility in the world] and the US Agency for International Development [a federal agency notorious for its ongoing collaborations with the CIA].

3. National Institute of Immunology. Located in India, "Major financiers are the Indian government, the Canadian International Development Research Centre and the Rockefeller Foundation."

4. The Contraceptive Development Program. This is US based, and is run on taxpayer monies.

5. The Center for Population Research. This is located at the National Institute of Child Health and Development, which is part of the US National Institutes of Health. This effort too is funded by taxpayer monies.

Sprenger mentions that universities in France, Germany, and Kenya, and the Medical Research Council in England are undertaking research and clinical trials with anti-fertility vaccines. Two European pharmaceutical firms, Schering in Germany and Organon in the Netherlands fund research in these vaccines.

One can see that this global research program is widespread

and involves a consensus about the goal of anti-fertility or sterilization on a mass level.

88

To show how far researchers will go in this direction, and at what cost to what we would call a natural human being, the anti-fertility vaccine researched by The Population Council, already in clinical trials, targets a hormone called GnRH. This hormone, responsible for releasing hCG, is itself made inside the hypothalamus, in the brain. GnRH has a range of functions. It fine-tunes steroid hormones, Sprenger writes. So this anti-fertility vaccine "brings the hormonal cascade to a total stand-still [and therefore] both male and female recipients need synthetic steroid hormone replacement..."

89

Journal paper.

Pediatrics, January 1996, pp.53 and 58, "Changing Levels of Measles Antibody Titers [concentrations] in Women and Children..." Authored by Laurie E. Markowitz et al.

First this: "An increasing proportion of children in the United States will respond to the measles vaccine at younger ages because of lower levels of passively acquired maternal measles antibodies."

And this: "The major reason that children fail to respond to the measles vaccine is the presence of passively acquired maternal antibodies."

In other words, a mother has developed natural antibodies [immune defense] against measles from her own childhood experience of the disease. She passes these antibodies on to her new baby, thus protecting for a time the baby against measles. This is all very clear and natural and easy to understand. However, from the vaccine manufacturer's point of view, it's a problem. Why? Because the mother's powerful antibodies against measles, in being passed to her baby, render useless the measle vaccine that could be given to the baby.

However, the vaccine makers are optimistic:

"Because of widespread use of the [measles] vaccine in the United States and high immunization levels after entry into school, most women of childbearing age in the United States now acquire measles immunity from vaccination, not wild measles virus infection. Because vaccination results in lower antibody titers [concentrations] than does natural infection, these women are likely to pass lower levels of the measles antibody to their infants."

More and more mothers, as a result of their own vaccinations against measles when they were children, now get their immunity against the disease from the vaccine, not from naturally experiencing measles and building up immune defenses that way. Vaccine-acquired immunity in the mothers is weaker than natural immunity. Therefore, these vaccinated mothers will pass fewer antibodies against measles on to their babies—and their babies will be able to respond to the measles vaccine.

If this seems absurd, it is. From several angles.

Most important, in the absence of vaccines, a child gets measles and experiences a full inflammatory response. This makes him stronger, this makes his immune system more capable.

When health officials mention that more very young children and babies are coming down with measles these days and therefore need the protection of the vaccine, they ignore the obvious fact that measles are visiting younger babies because their mothers are passing fewer antibodies on to them to protect them—and THIS is because their mothers were vaccinated and are not giving them the more powerful natural antibodies.

There are even more absurd and more basic problems, but we will leave them for another time.

Here is another quote from the *Pediatrics* paper:

"Our data indicate that, in the future, when virtually all women of child-bearing age will have vaccine-induced immunity, the recommended age for vaccination may be able to be lowered without diminishing vaccine efficacy."

This is a perfect example of introducing a synthetic replacement-version of natural events—when the natural events are without difficulties.

Add into this the very frequent bad vaccine reactions that occur with all immunizations, and you have a prescription for disaster.

But the drive to make synthetic life processes and $ increases among the corporate generals.

90

Of course, whether anyone is actually helped by such a vaccine is beside the point.

The vaccine makers are looking for clinical signs that their vaccine is causing the body to make antibodies.

Antibodies, however, are just part of the surveillance system of the whole immune system, and many people who are vaccinated and then show antibodies are not, in fact, protected.

They go on to get the disease.

We are now in a shadow world, in a charade of "clinical markers" and "positive signs" and "expected reactions," all of which have been assembled to show that a medicine or a treatment or a vaccine is working ... but in truth such indications may be irrelevant.

Which makes up what a court would call depraved indifference to life.

91

To flesh out US population-control policy a little further:

President Richard Nixon, in a classified National Security Council Memorandum, number 970, on "The New US Foreign Assistance Program," moved the whole issue of population control to major status in US foreign policy.

Following up, his Secretary of State, Henry Kissinger, on April 24, 1974, sent a memorandum to the secretary of agriculture, the secretary of defense, the director of the CIA, the deputy secretary of state and the director of AID (the Agency for International Development).

Kissinger asked for a study to be done concerning "the impact of world population growth on US security and overseas interests."

The study was done. It was issued—confidentially, of course—on December 10, 1974.

In late 1975, the National Security Council wrote a directive which essentially made the conclusions of the study into US foreign policy.

The study said that a power shift could soon occur because Third World nations were expanding their populations. Two prominent examples mentioned were Brazil and Nigeria. (Their currencies and economies are now in shambles.)

It discussed the US military/industrial need for minerals in the Third World, and the possibility that "[local] revolutionary actions" there could bring about "expropriation of foreign [US] interests."

The study recommended that the US government link its foreign aid to proof from key nations that they were lowering their birth rates. It also recommended major media efforts in these countries aimed at getting people to have fewer children.

92

Suppose that one day in the not too distant future, scientists find a reliable way to clone a liver or a heart or a leg.

How likely is it that this technology will be exported to the slums of Calcutta?

It is one thing to say that a man drives around Beverly Hills in a Rolls and stops in for lunch at the Polo Lounge, while another man in Kampala who is starving drinks water that has been pumped in directly from sewage without processing.

It is another thing to say that a man in Beverly Hills who reaches 60 can have, as a matter of course, a clone of his own heart transplanted in two hours, while a man with a diseased heart in the slums of Sao Paulo cannot, under any circumstances, obtain the same favor.

Perhaps these two examples are actually almost the same. But because we still retain a vague residual feeling that healing should be available to all, we see, in the second case, a sign that the world of the rich and the world of the poor would be irretrievably split.

How can a world like that survive?

And, therefore, how far a leap is it for certain influential and very rich people, fearful of their position, to want to eliminate the have-nots altogether?

93

Proponents of GE food say that the corporations are Jesus Christs who will feed the world, that the world cannot be fed any other way.

This is clearly false.

Many systems of agriculture exist which, if practiced well and widely, would alleviate hunger in every country.

Food does not have to be GE to work.

Questions about the effects of GE food on humans, which of course have never been answered, are well illustrated by the authors of the book, *Genetically Engineered Foods*. They use the 1989 story of the tryptophan scandal.

This amino acid, sold widely as a food supplement, was produced by many companies, but one company chose to manufacture it by GE. Bacteria were engineered to produce tryptophan, but when the bacteria did they made such large amounts it caused a reaction within themselves, and a new toxin was secreted in tiny, tiny amounts.

Apparently that toxin caused the syndrome named eosinophilia-myalgia. It killed 37 people. 1500 had partial paralysis. 5000 became ill.

If minute toxic changes like this occurred within GE crops, it would be very difficult to trace.

94

In the major report, *Excessive Force: Power, Politics, and Population Control*, by the Washington DC group, Information Project for Africa, Inc., the authors discuss what may become a widespread form of sterilization in the world: the quinacrine pellet.

"When inserted into a woman's uterus, quinacrine inflicts burn-like injuries, causing sufficient damage to bring about permanent infertility. Thus it promises to be the long-sought non-surgical technique for permanent sterilization, a fact which was not overlooked by the authors of a [May 29] 1989 commentary in the *International Journal of Gynecology and Obstetrics* who asserted that the drug could potentially increase female sterilizations in India by about a million a year. Quinacrine has several known side effects—among them 'toxic psychosis,' which means chemically- induced insanity." (See "Delivery Systems for Applying Quinacrine as a Tubal Closing Agent" by Robert G. Wheeler, in *Female Transcervical Sterilization*, Hagerstown, Maryland, Harper and Row, 1983)

95

An *AP* story, "Birth-Control Vaccine is Reported in India," appeared in the *Boston Globe* on October 10, 1992.

New Delhi: "Scientists said yesterday they have created the first birth-control shot for women, effective for an entire year ... [after which] a booster shot is needed.

"The main element of the injection is beta-hCG, which triggers the production of antibodies to hCG, or human chorionic gonadotropin, a hormone essential in sustaining pregnancy, scientists said."

96

On January 6, 1998, National Public Radio, on its *All Things Considered*, had reporter Joe Palca interview a physicist and

fertility researcher from Chicago, Richard Seed. Seed said he was raising money to start a human clone clinic in the Chicago area.

Author of a 1983 article in the *Journal of the American Medical Association* on egg transference from a fertile woman to an infertile woman, Seed said that he and his colleagues were prepared to start a human cloning attempt within 90 days.

This method involves the removal of DNA from a woman's egg and the replacement of it with the DNA of the person to be cloned.

There are unknowns in this method.

97

Dream conversation.

"Look at these regions on the globe marked in blue."

"Very unproductive countries."

"Not only do they have almost non-existent GNPs, they don't have a lot of natural resources. So we accelerate our depopulation efforts there."

"And then?"

"Repopulate the areas with companies ready to go, ready to set up towns of employees run according to company rules."

"Create economies out of nothing."

"Exactly. And eventually, we may be able to synthesize part of the population."

"In what way?"

"By cloning. Create workers according to specs."

"Sounds technologically difficult."

"Even if it takes a hundred years."

"A future."

"Yes. Imagine it."

"So we would have a two-level research effort."

"How so?"

"On the one hand, we talk about cloning babies as an option, as a reproductive right for a woman. Couch it all in terms of freedom and choice. With all the research that comes out of this, we use the best methods for what you're suggesting. Mass cloning according to specs."

"Of course we'd have secret research projects going on at the same time."

"Under Pentagon contracts."

"Eventually we could replace populations in nations that don't seem to respond to the consumer economy as a paradigm."

"Depopulate and repopulate."

"There are now only 800 million people in the global marketplace. This would be a way to jump-start that. The biggest corporations are on permanent slowdown in their assembly lines. They can actually produce products for the planet two times over."

"Yes. We would also depopulate the areas where indigenous peoples could cause too much disruption to the corporations that have taken over their lands. I mean, it's all an experiment, right?"

98

In 1987, journalist Robert Lederer wrote about a vaccine against hog cholera. The serum was developed from pig blood which turned out to be tainted with African Swine Fever (ASF).

"Thus," Lederer suggests, "during mass [pig] vaccination programs, the tainted vaccine prevented hog cholera but also induced ASF on a mass scale."

Ben Dupuy, editor of New York's *Haiti Progress*, told Lederer he believed the hog cholera vaccine was intentionally introduced into Haiti to blast the poor-peasant infrastructure. With the death of their pigs during the ensuing ASF epidemic of 1979, Dupuy maintains peasants were forced to pay $100 apiece for new pigs brought in from the US. Of course, they couldn't afford this. The idea was to drive peasants off their land into low-paying urban jobs and, from the outside, establish a new Haitian economy (US controlled) of huge farms and factories.

In this regard, Lederer also cites an article from the *New York Native*, December 17, 1984, in which Jane Teas (Harvard School of Public Health) remarks that ASF first broke out in Haiti in a well-populated valley that was due to be flooded, as part of a hydroelectric dam project.

99

Lederer, in a 1987 article in *Covert Action* (Number 28, "Precedents for AIDS?"), summarizes a series of tests on prisoners which could rightly be called chemical warfare:

"From 1965 to 1968, 70 prisoners, mostly black, at Holmesburg State Prison in Philadelphia, were the subjects of tests by Dow Chemical Company of the effects of dioxin, the highly toxic chemical contaminant of Agent Orange. Their skins were deliberately exposed to large doses and then monitored to watch the results. According to the doctor in charge, Albert Kligman, a University of Pennsylvania dermatologist, several subjects developed lesions which 'lasted for four to seven months, since no effort was made to speed healing by active treatment.' At a 1980 federal Environmental Protection Agency hearing where the experiments came to light, Kligman testified that no follow-up was done on subjects for possible development of cancer. This was the second such experiment commissioned by Dow, the previous one carried out on 51 'volunteers,' believed also to have been prisoners."

100

NA Mitchison, writing in the journal *Current Opinion in Immunology* ("Gonadotropic Vaccines"), 1990, volume 2, p.725:

"At present, the most advanced birth control vaccines are based on human chorionic gonadotropin (hCG) ... [after] 2 decades of development... "

"I have been told that India's next 5-year plan makes

provision for their introduction [the hCG vaccines] as part of the national birth control program."

101

From *The Lancet*, June 11, 1988, pp.1295-1298, "Clinical Trials of a WHO Birth Control Vaccine," by WR Jones, et al:
"Thirty surgically sterilised female workers, divided into five equal groups for different vaccine doses, received two intramuscular injections six weeks apart. Over a six-month follow-up there were no important adverse reactions, and potentially contraception levels of antibodies to hCG developed in all subjects."

"Since 1974, the Task Force on Birth Control Vaccines of the World Health Organization (WHO) ... has promoted the development of a contraceptive vaccine directed against the pregnancy hormone human chorionic gonadotropin (hCG)."

Again, WHO does not develop a vaccine like this for the independent woman in Shaker Heights who doesn't want to get pregnant. We are talking about mass injections over wide populations.

102

The Lancet, 4 June 1988, p.1272:
"During the recent National Immunisation Campaign (vaccination for childhood diseases and tetanus toxoid for pregnant women), in some villages [of Thailand] the women escaped and hid in the bushes thinking that they were going to be given injections to stop them having children."

103

From the *LA Times*, February 18, 1999, by *Times* legal writer Henry Weinstein:
"In the latest front of Holocaust-related litigation, a federal class-action suit was filed Wednesday on behalf of survivors

of Nazi death camps, alleging that Bayer AG, the giant German-owned chemical and pharmaceutical company, participated in cruel medical experiments by the infamous Dr. Josef Mengele.

"The suit ... alleges that Bayer 'monitored and supervised those experiments, and used them as a form of research and development for its corporate benefit.'

"... On Tuesday, Bayer AG was among a group of a dozen German companies that said they would participate in a $1.7 billion fund to compensate individuals who had been used as slave labor and forced labor during World War II.

"The plan was announced by German Chancellor Gerhard Schroeder, who said a primary role of the fund was 'to counter lawsuits, particularly class-action lawsuits, and to remove the basis of the campaign being led against German industry and our country.'

"... The named plaintiff in the new suit ... is Eva Mozes Kor, one of 1,500 sets of twins subjected to grotesque experiments at the Auschwitz concentration camp during the Holocaust. The research on twins, which Mengele directed, was designed to investigate the effect of numerous bacteria, chemicals and viruses on the human body ... Frequently, the Nazis decided that to complete the research it was necessary to kill both twins so that doctors could conduct autopsies..."

"... According to the suit, 'Bayer provided toxic chemicals to the Nazis ... Some of those experiments involved injecting concentration camp inmates with toxic chemicals and germs known to cause diseases in order to test the effectiveness of various drugs manufactured by Bayer.'

"... According to the suit, post-World War II publications reported that Bayer participated in the experiments, 'giving orders to [Nazi] SS Major Dr. Helmuth Vetter, who was associated with Bayer and who was stationed in several concentration camps. Dr. Vetter experimented in Auschwitz with medications ... [that] were administered to healthy inmates who had first been rendered ill from infections that were intentionally administered through pills, powders, injections or enemas.'

"Vetter was sentenced to death by an American military

court in 1947 and executed in 1949."

104

Force and deception are foundation-stones of tyrannies. Around the world these tyrannies compete and also join together to form great secret empires. Secret? Only because their publics in the industrial nations do not believe that governments and transnational corporations are One. The governments are the enforcers; the corporations are the profit makers. In other circles this is called organized crime.

Epilogue

Here are several more examples of boggling stories which somehow do not make it on to the nightly news.

These stories would be "bad for corporate business," and therefore bad for the careers of the anchors, editors and producers who permitted them to be aired and repeated.

1. On July 2, 1997, an extraordinary letter was sent to Jeff Green, head of Citizens for Safe Drinking Water, in San Diego.

It came from a union, the National Federation of Federal Employees, local 2050, based in Washington DC.

The subject is fluoridation of community and city drinking water. Here is the letter in full. It contains explosive points:

> "I am pleased to report that our union, Local 2050, National Federation of Federal Employees, has voted to co-sponsor the California citizens' petition to prohibit fluoridation of which your organization is the sponsor. Our union represents, and is comprised of, the scientists, lawyers, engineers and other professionals at the headquarters of the US Environmental Protection Agency here in Washington, D.C.
>
> "A vote of the membership was taken at a meeting during which Professor Paul Connett and Dr. Robert Carton made presentations, respectively, on the recent toxicological and epidemiological evidence developed on fluoride and past actions (and their bases) of Local 2050 with respect to fluoride in drinking water. The membership vote was unanimous in favor of co-sponsorship.
>
> "It is our hope that our so-sponsorship will have a beneficial effect on the health and welfare of all Californians by helping to keep their drinking water free

of a chemical substance for which there is substantial evidence of adverse health effects and, contrary to public perception, virtually no evidence of significant benefits.

"These judgements are based, in part, on animal studies of the toxicity of fluoride coupled with the human epidemiology studies which corroborate them, and the studies of rates of decayed, missing, and filled teeth in the United States (fluoridated and non-fluoridated communities) versus non-fluoridated European countries.

"Our members' review of the body of evidence over the last eleven years, including animal and human epidemiology studies, indicate a causal link between fluoride/fluoridation and cancer, genetic damage, neurological impairment and bone pathology. Of particular concern are recent epidemiology studies linking fluoride exposures to lower IQ in children.

"As professionals who are charged with assessing the safety of drinking water, we conclude that the health and welfare of the public is not served by the addition of this substance to the public water supply.

"Best wishes to you and your organization for success in keeping what would otherwise be a hazardous waste of the fertilizer industry from being disposed of in California's drinking water supplies.

"Sincerely,

> J. William Hirzy, Ph.D.,
> Senior Vice-President."

Note that fluorides are called a hazardous waste from a non-related corporate activity.

And if that hazardous waste results in "cancer, genetic damage, neurological impairment, and bone pathology," there are ready medical labels and sub-labels for these conditions which serve to confuse and divert public attention from the real cause—and there are medical "treatments," which themselves are toxic and create even more distance between the original corporate cause and public awareness. That is the way the game is often played, and we have to realize it.

2. On the Monsanto corporation website for the UK (www.monsanto.co.uk), there is a menu item called Biotech Primer. The question listed under that item is: "What about consumer information?" Here is Monsanto's answer:

> "Labelling helps consumers decide what they buy. Decisions about the labelling of foods containing ingredients from genetically modified crops are made by the European Union and the UK food industry labels many of these foods.
>
> "In order to help improve public understanding of modern biotechnology and genetic modification, the food industry in this country is working to keep consumers better informed. Public information is a priority and we at Monsanto are working to achieve this through a variety of different approaches."

Presumably there is some intrinsic difference between American and British humans, because in America Monsanto has done everything it can to prevent mandatory labels which would tell consumers whether they are buying GE food.

Maybe the Brits have a gene which makes it necessary for them to know, and the Americans don't, so they can live in the dark.

3. In Los Angeles, the Foundation for Advancements in Science and Education released an astounding report (spring 1998): "Pesticide Exports from US Ports, 1995-1996." The report noted that, "Despite a quarter century on the verge of export reform, American policy makers have not acted to stop the export of pesticides forbidden in the US."

Here is the abstract of the report:

> "Analyzing data from US Customs shipping records, researchers at the Foundation for Advancements in Science and Education found that more than 338 million

pounds of hazardous pesticides were exported from US ports during 1995 and 1996. The majority went to destinations in the developing world. During this period, at least 21 million pounds of pesticides which are forbidden to be used in the United States were exported. These estimates must be regarded as conservative in view of the fact that specific names were omitted from the shipping records for nearly two-thirds of the pesticides exported. In fact, between 1992 and 1996, more than 2 billion pounds of pesticides left US ports with their specific chemical names omitted from publicly accessible shipping records—a rate well over 500 tons per day."

4. Ronnie Cummins, in issue #17 of *Food Bytes*, writing on "Global Resistance Against Monsanto and GE," reports that February 12, 1999 page-one stories in the British press exposed the health dangers of genetically engineered potatoes. Dr. Arpad Pustazi — and a backup panel of "20 international scientists" — have come forward with a series of animal studies which show the potatoes caused immune-system damage, and damage to "thymuses, kidneys, spleens, and guts."

This is just the sort of research that could set off a public panic.

Just after Dr. Pustazi announced his first set of findings in August, 1999, he was fired from his job at a government research facility, the Rowett Institute in Scotland.

A Final Note on AIDS

Looking back on *AIDS INC.*, a book I wrote in 1987-88, I now see that AIDS is the best example I have found of the perverse depicting of human misery by large interests for their own protection and $.

Start with this. When Rachel Carson wrote her book, *Silent Spring*, she provoked outrage at the underlying idea that major American companies could poison the water, ground, and air of this world and then lie through their teeth about it.

Eventually, however, people began to see that corporations were not models of civilized behavior.

The same evolution of public opinion is occurring in the field of mainstream medicine. It is now more widely known that huge segments of the medical profession—see Peter Breggin's *Toxic Psychiatry*, for example—are entirely grounded in arbitrary descriptions of illnesses which do not even exist. People are suffering and dying, but not because of the fancy-named conditions which they are said to have.

Attention Deficit Disorder (ADD) has never been found to be a disease with a physical cause. Instead, it turns out to be a grab-bag of behaviors which teachers and parents find objectionable in children. Add to that actual nutritional deficiencies and toxic conditions caused by allergies, serious reactions to food additives and to vaccines and medical drugs, to pesticides, to excessive amounts of refined sugar, and you have what ADD actually is. A group of conditions stemming from various causes and combinations of causes which have been falsely welded together under one name with one treatment, Ritalin, a cheap speed-type drug.

This absurd ADD diagnosis and this treatment achieves several ends, if we stop looking at the world through rose-colored glasses. It brings in lots of dollars to Novartis, which makes Ritalin, and it protects food corporations from giant liability in causing illness in children. It also lets teachers and parents off the hook ... they no longer need to feel challenged or responsible for the way their children are acting. Leave it to the doctor—who, frankly, doesn't know what hell he is doing.

A rather disgusting picture, all in all. Small amounts of dexedrine or cocaine or possibly procaine could, for a short time, improve a child's concentration. That's the initial effect of many drugs. But we aren't rushing to buy cocaine for children. We know better. No, instead, we're worshipping at the fount of the white coats, the doctors, with their obfuscating language and their backups of huge pharmaceutical firms who sell programs of treatment which are harmful. Which include Ritalin, pharmacologically the same as the amphetamines

In the case of AIDS, it turns out that many interests are served by welding together huge and diverse kinds of immune-suppression around the planet, tying them all to a germ called HIV and calling "it" AIDS. Money is made for Glaxo-Wellcome, the British firm that makes and sells AZT. Manufacturers of immune suppression—everything from toxic medical drugs to pesticides to disgusting public opinion rallied against gay men—benefit from the smokescreen called AIDS.

And worst of all, by hypnotizing and terrifying people all over the world about HIV, and by failing to diagnose what, in any given case, really is causing the depression of a person's immune system, you close to the door to a cure and you sentence that person to a life of pain, or to death.

That's how "advantageous theories" can cause death, and that's how forms of poisoning which could bring legal liability down on certain elite corporations is diverted into other channels, where exalted experts hold sway, let the real perpetrators off the hook, befuddle everyone with their so-called expertise, and wave their syringes and prescription pads as societies fall apart.

Like it or not, that's the story.

Acknowledgments

To researchers Paul Borraccia, Ronnie Cummins, Tarik Ricard, Keidi Obi Awadu, and James A Miller. To Bonnie Lange, David Sielaff, Erica McGrath, Grafy, Miki Jo Burg, Nancy Melton, at The Truth Seeker. To She and He Who Remember, to Keith and John at the late great Deep River Books. To Ida Honoroff, a cosmic force. To Ann and Ralph for their kindnesses, and to Tom Davis. To Bruce, Rockie, and NCARX. To all the people at The Great Boycott, especially Barbara, Frank, Robert, and Ignacio.

Is your solution to what is in these pages simply casting a vote for a Republican or a Democrat and then going home? Do you really think so?

Feel free to donate your time to any of the several fine organizations mentioned in this book: e.g., the Pure Food Campaign (www.purefood.com) and The Great Boycott (ph: 310-281-1927: http://home.earthlink.net/~alto/boycott.html).

There is another group, the Alliance For Child Protection From Toxic Abuse, that does excellent research and education. They can be called at 818-780-3330. Their mailing address is PO Box 55335, Sherman Oaks, CA 91413.

My publisher and I have begun a project called Creating the Future. For this, contact the Truth Seeker at 800-321-9054.

End Notes

Introduction

The best books on IG Farben I have found are *The Crime and Punishment of IG Farben* by Joseph Borkin (Free Press, New York, 1978) and *The Devil's Chemists* by Josiah DuBois and Edward Johnson (Beacon Press, Boston, 1952, and S.J.R. Saunders, Toronto.)

But one should also read *Trading With the Enemy* by Charles Higham and *Du Pont: Behind the Nylon Curtain* by Gerard Colby.

1

The apparatus of denial on the part of anchors like Dan Rather, Tom Brokaw, and Peter Jennings would probably contain fragments of ideas like: "the human being is a limited creature to begin with" and "we're bringing more news to the public than they've ever had before." Sub-text? "The foreign policy of the United States for the past 200 years involves inflicting physical and economic pain on all peoples who would obstruct—by their desire for freedom—investment in and control of their lands and persons by American corporations, but who the hell can put THAT on the air every night?"

2

Higham, *Trading With the Enemy*, published by Barnes and Noble, New York, 1995.

3

Biotechnology's Bitter Harvest, a report of the Biotechnology Working Group, 1990, funded in part by the CS Fund in California. This report lists the largest pesticide companies in the world: Monsanto, Dow/Elanco, Du Pont, Imperial Chemical Industries, Bayer, Hoechst, Rhone Poulenc and Ciba Geigy (now Novartis). It reveals that all these companies have been deeply involved in researching genetically engineered food seeds, which will result in, among other curses, crops much more "tolerant" to herbicides.

4

See *Toxic Sludge Is Good For You*, by John Stauber and Sheldon Rampton, Common Courage Press, 1995. It will change your life.

5

Du Pont Dynasty, Colby, Lyle Stuart Publishing, Seacaucus, New Jersey, 1984 edition. In *Toxic Sludge*, Stauber describes how Colby's book was stopped from becoming a best seller.

6

Phone the excellent organization Alive and Well Alternatives at 877-92-ALIVE, and www.aliveandwell.org on the internet.

8–9

See my *AIDS INC.*, Human Energy Press, Foster City, CA, 1988. Distributed by The Truth Seeker, San Diego. The information concerning The San Francisco Men's Study comes from personal interviews.

11

See the excellent *Psychiatrists—the Men Behind Hitler*, by Roder, Kubillus and Burwell. Freedom Publishing, Los Angeles, 1995.

12

Global Dreams: Imperial Corporations and the New World Order, by Richard Barnet and John Cavanaugh, Simon and Schuster, New York, 1994.

13

Reclaiming Our Health, by John Robbins, HJ Kramer Publishers, Tiburon, CA, 1996.

14

Toxic Psychiatry by Peter Breggin, St. Martin's Press, New York, 1994. This is a heroic book which should be in every hotel room in America. And in every home.

15

Townsend Letter for Doctors, June 1993.

16

Article: "The rBGH Scandals," by the Pure Food Campaign and the Campaign For Food Safety, 860 Highway 61, Little Marais, Minnesota, 55614. http://www.purefood.org

17

Article: "Monsanto Concealed Potential rBGH Hazards From Public," by Peter Montague, *Rachel's Environment and Health Weekly*, Oct. 22, 1998, Annapolis, MD.

18

Article: "Monsanto Protects Itself From Product Liability," *Rachel's Hazardous Waste News*, #383, Mar. 31, 1994. Same address.

19

Article: "Hormonal Rage: Monsanto Spikes a Florida TV Story About Its Bovine Growth Hormone," by Jeannette Batz, Pure Food Campaign.

21

Physician's Desk Reference.

25

Corporate Crimes in the Pharmaceutical Industry, by John Braithwaite, Routledge and Kegan Paul, 1984.

28

A wonderful information gathering organization: Health Action International, summary of the SMON case, by Andrew Chetley, 1993, Amsterdam.

29

The excerpt from Butler's speech is printed in *Prevailing Winds Magazine*, issue #2, Santa Barbara, CA.

30

Article: "Corporate Royalty," by Karl Davies, People Against Corporate Takeover, Northampton, MA.
www.ratical.org/corporations/CorpRoyalty.html

31

C-Span 2 carried this press conference.

32

Taking Care of Business: Citizenship and the Charter of Incorporation by Richard Grossman, published by Charter/Ink. The organization is CSPP, Box 806, Cambridge, MA 02140. This booklet is truly groundbreaking work.

33

Genetically Engineered Foods: Are They Safe? by Laura Ticciati and Robin Ticciati, Keats Publishing, New Canaan CT, 1998. Give it to your friends. It is a remarkable work of compression.

34

Article: untitled—a survey of activism taken against GE food, by Ronnie Cummins, in *Food Bytes* #15, Campaign For Food Safety. See Pure Food Campaign website address.

35

Higham, *Trading With the Enemy.*

36

Utopia or Oblivion, Buckminster Fuller, Overlook Press, New York, 1969.

37

Article: "NAFTA Blues," by Bill Medaille and Andrew Wheat, *Multinational Monitor*, December 1997.

38–39

War Is a Racket, by Smedley Butler, Round Table Press, New York, 1935.

40–41

Higham, *Trading With the Enemy.*

42

See info sheet from the Nestle Boycott, Friends of the Breastfeeding Society. ph: 519-327-8785.

44

Health Action International monographs on toxic pharmaceuticals, Amsterdam.

45

The Compleat Mother Journal, Minot, ND.

46

Colby, *Du Pont Dynasty.*

47–49

For statements about Du Pont, see Colby.

50

Higham, *Trading With the Enemy.*

52

Trilateralism, ed. by Holly Sklar, South End Press, Boston, 1980. Also, re Nicaragua, see *Dollars and Dictators,* Tom Barry et al, Grove Press, New York, 1983; and *Endless Enemies* by Jonathan Kwitney, Congdon and Weed Publishers, New York, 1984.

53

Multinational Monitor, October, 1998.

54

Multinational Monitor, Jan/Feb 1998.

56

Rachel's Environment and Health Weekly, #304, "Free Trade, part 2," PO Box 5036, Annapolis, MD 21403.

57

Multinational Monitor, Jan/Feb 1998.

58

Multinational Monitor, Sept. 1998.

59

Multinational Monitor, Jan/Feb 1998.

60

Psychiatrists—the Men Behind Hitler.

61

About Ritalin, see *Toxic Psychiatry*, Peter Breggin. Also, *Talking Back to Ritalin* by Peter Breggin, Common Courage Press, Monroe, Maine, 1998.

See the *PDR* for quotes and information on drugs mentioned in this section.

62

For AZT, see my *AIDS INC.* Also consult Aive and Well for copies of John Lauritsen's groundbreaking *Poison By Prescription: The AZT Story.* In a sane world, Lauritsen and

Breggin would have received several Pulitzers by now.

64

Campaign For Food Safety, Little Marais, Minnesota. Also, *The Gene Exchange* issue for fall/winter 1998. www.ucsusa.org

65

September 4, 1998 issue of *Congressional Quarterly*.

66

NORML, Washington DC.

73–79

See *Genetically Engineered Foods: Are They Safe?* by Ticciati. Again, this book will properly rattle the cage of any mainstream American. At the same time, it is an expert work for people wanting an overview of a subject they already dimly perceive.

82

Global Dreams, Barnet and Cavanaugh.

91

"Population Control, a National Security Issue," by Elizabeth Sobo, in the *National Catholic Reporter*, Nov. 23, 1990.

98

See ch.28, *AIDS INC.*

99

Ch.26, *AIDS INC.*

See ch.25, AIDS INC.

Ch.26, AIDS INC.